WAKE UP!
TAKE THIS JOB!

Lifting You Out Of The Unemployment Statistics

SAMUEL S. AGHOMI

PRAISE FOR
WAKE UP! TAKE THIS JOB!

"Very well researched and written book. Practical, informative, appealing, daring and helpful. A must read and actionable book for all Nigerian Youths and Adults"
-Fred Onakpoya

This book "Wake up! Take this job! Is very inspiring and motivating. Every reader will find it an invaluable treasure. It's practical and worth owning.
-Elder. Hampo A. Cy
Principal, Step Forward Group of Schools, Warri

"Readers will find the book (Wake up! Take this job!) useful, as it is rich in knowledge and thought. There is no doubt; it will provide the needed inspiration catalyst and springboard that the youths require to break the yoke of unemployment"
-Dr. F.O. Money
Former Ag. Provost, College of Education, Warri
Former Provost, College of Physical and Health Education, Mosoger, Delta State

"...thought provoking book."
-William Ofishe
Head of Department (HOD)
Department of Business Education,

"In times like this, youths must face the realities of life instead of a life of mirage. WAKE UP! TAKE THIS JOB! Moved me deeply, a gripping reality. It will transform your life's journey."
-Engr. Emmanuel Osiaje
President, Delta State Baptist Youth Conference (DSBYC)

WAKE UP! TAKE THIS JOB!
Copyright© 2013

SAMUEL S. AGHOMI

ISBN:9789785207804

Published and Printed in Nigeria by:

Baptist Press (Nig.) Limited, Ibadan

All Right Reserved

No portion of this book maybe used without the written permission of the author/publisher, with exception of brief excerpts in Magazine, articles, reviews, etc
For further information or permission, address

**Baptist Press (Nig.) Limited,
P.M.B 5071
Ibadan, Oyo State**

All scriptural quotations are from the King James Version (KJV) of the Holy Bible, other versions used include:

WEB:	World English bible
NIV:	New International version
AMP:	Amplified Version
TLB:	The Living Bible

Cover Designed by: Graphic Unit, Rateda Printing Press, Warri
08037403094, 08023301513

"Deep within man dwells those slumbering powers; power that would astonish him, that he never dreamed of possessing; forces that would revolutionize his life if aroused and put into action"
-Orison Swett Marden

"There is a power within you. A power that is invisible, intangible, but completely real. A power that can transform you so dramatically that under its influence and guidance you can become an entirely new person, stronger, more confident, better balanced, more energetic, more resilient, more capable of coping with ever-increasing complexity of modern living"
-Norman Vincent Peale

Wake up! Take This Job!

CONTENTS

Dedication
Acknowledgment
Foreword
Introduction

CHAPTER ONE
BREAKING THE GLASS CEILING

CHAPTER TWO
NEW DEFINITION, NEW HORIZON

CHAPTER THREE
THE ROAD TO INDEPENDENCE

CHAPTER FOUR
ADJUST YOUR ATTITUDE

CHAPTER FIVE
THE PRODUCTS OF A LOADED BRAIN

CHAPTER SIX
PERSONAL REVENUE GENERATION

CHAPTER SEVEN
LEARNING FOR LIVING

CHAPTER EIGHT
STEPPING IN AS AN ENTREPRENEUR

CHAPTER NINE

Wake up! Take This Job!

THE DIGITAL SHIFT

CHAPTER TEN
DEALING WITH IMMOBILIZERS

CHAPTER ELEVEN
DEALING WITH LAZINESS AND EXCUSES

CHAPTER TWELVE
BREAKING THE FORCE OF INERTIA

CHAPTER THIRTEEN
THE JOB SHIFT

CHAPTER FOURTEEN
ORDINARY JOBS WITH EXTRAORDINARY POTENTIALS

CHAPTER FIFTEEN
INDISPENSABLE REQUIREMENTS FOR ALL ORDINARY JOB PROVIDERS

CHAPTER SIXTEEN
THE GAINS OF ENGAGING IN COMMON JOBS

FINAL WORD

Bibliography

Dedication

To the teeming Nigerian graduates who are still struggling to find their place in the scheme of things.

Acknowledgement

This book is the product of a journey; the journey is the product of part of my life's journey. Like every successful journey, there are a number of wonderful people who contributed in countless ways to my experience in writing this book.

My gratitude goes to my beautiful and lovely wife Elo-oghene Precious who consistently encouraged me to write and finish this book.

The manuscript was first read by Elder Hampo A. Cy, the Principal of Step Forward Group of Schools, Warri and Mr. Fred Onakpoya, an embodiment of wisdom and a mentor, who made several corrections and constructive criticisms which eventually pave the way for a more elaborate and detailed research about the subject covered in this book.

The indispensable role that Mr. Edward E. Ukeredi Director/Principal of Delta Careers College, Warri, has played in my life and in the transformation of this book from an idea into a life changing material that you now hold in your hands is worth appreciating. Sir, you have been a father, role model and mentor. Your desire to see that I succeed in life is deeply appreciated, you have being a great blessing to me and my family, thank you.

To my spiritual father, my Pastor, Rev. Bill Awaritoma, the Senior Pastor of Estate Baptist Church, Warri and his lovely wife Mrs. Christy Awaritoma, thank you for your unwavering support and the invaluable role you have played and you are still playing in my life.

Thank you to Dr. (Barr) S.E. Efuetanu Director/Proprietor of Step-Forward Group of Schools for your encouragement and support.

Wake up! Take This Job!

Thank you to Dr. F.O. Money the former Provost of College of Physical and Health Education, Mosogar for finding time to read through this book and making invaluable technical input.

Thank you to Mr. W.O. Ofishe of the Head of Department of Business Education, College of Education, Warri and the Coordinator of Nigeria Institute of Management (NIM), Warri for finding time to read through this book and making invaluable input and suggestions.

Thank you to Mrs. Hannah Omeru of Rute International Schools, Warri for your encouragement and support.

Thank you to Mr. Michael Aigbokie and his dear wife Mrs. Stella Aigbokie for your encouragement and support, the extent of your generosity and kindness towards me and my family is sincerely appreciated.

Thank you to Rev. Abos O. Willie, Chairman, Youth Wing Christian Association of Nigeria (YOWICAN) Delta State for believing in me.

Thank you to Engr. Emmanuel Osiaje, President Delta State Baptist Youth Convention (DSBYC), for being a big brother, for your encouragement, support and also allowing me to tap into your wealth of experience in youth affairs and finally for finding time to read through the manuscript and making priceless input.

Thank you to Barrister Ben Oji for squeezing out time from your busy schedule to read through this book and for helping to shape it and make it more reader friendly.

Four of my friends in particular played important role in helping me conceptualize this book, they are Anthony Futughe, Osazuwa Ohen, Rabome Avre and Owen, I am grateful to you guys for standing by me through out the period of writing this book.

My profound gratitude goes to everyone at the Baptist Press, Ibadan for an excellent work. I particularly, appreciate the Press

Wake up! Take This Job!

Editor Sis. Bunmi for her professionalism and commitment to see that this book is published. Thank you.

Finally, to Mrs. Kehinde Dorcas Onuwaje, I want to say thank you for exposing me to the details involved in making an excellent book and for your timely support. To Mr Edirin Ipopo Edgar for being a professional photographer, I say a big thank you. To my brother and friend Mr. Kingsley Chukwusa for standing by me, I say thank you. To Mr. Gbenga Olatunji (G.O) of the Graphic Unit, Rateda Printing Press Warri, thank you for designing a beautiful front cover for this book. To Ayo Olowookun and my friends at Factor A⁺ Business Centre in College of Education, Warri, I say a big thank you.

Foreword

Samuel S. Aghomi has literally shaken every sleeping reader of this book to wake up. The book x-rays the problems of joblessness and proffers solutions. Joblessness though a serious problem, is a human problem. And there is also a human solution to the problem.

"**Wake up! Take this job!**" is down to earth on the issue of joblessness. I completely agree with the author that there should be no reason why anybody should be jobless. If you are jobless, it means you have a problem; and your problem has been x-rayed in this book. A jobless person may consider himself as a failure but according to Mark Twain: *"there are a thousand excuses for failure but never a good reason"*. Mark Twain therefore does not believe in failure. I also do not believe in failure. There is therefore, no justification for joblessness.

The author, in this book, helps you to come out of your shell. He helps you to appreciate the fact that you can become whatever you want to become if you believe in yourself. Not only does he share his personal experience with you, but he also gives you practical example as to what to do to make a living. After all, what is the end of education? Pestalozzi describes the end of education as *"not a perfection in the accomplishments of the school, but fitness for life; not the acquirement of habits of blind obedience and prescribed diligence, but a preparation for independent action."* Yes, Pestalozzi believed that education is fitness for life and a preparation for action; an action which could sustain you. This

Wake up! Take This Job!

book should help you to make your education meaningful and purposeful.

I have found this book to be very informative, instructive and very educative. It is a book that should be read by all school leavers, right from Junior school to University. It is a book I will recommend to all even those who are gainfully employed; especially to our youths who are looking for jobs, which are not available. Every home needs this book. You are holding in your hands an invaluable TREASURE.

I wish you the best.

Emmanuel E. Ukeredi
Principal & Proprietor,
Delta Careers College
Ugboroke - Warri, Nigeria

Introduction

The date is 3rd July, 2010. I was on my way back to Warri, from Ibadan a south western city in Nigeria after completion of the National Youth Service Scheme (NYSC). As I journeyed back to Warri, my eyes were soaked in tears, I thought of all the precious people that I met, that I would miss; my heart was also filled with divers thought. Thoughts of what next to do, where to start from, where to stay and what the future holds ran through my mind intermittently. My heart was bleeding, tears were dripping and my pocket was empty.

Why was I emotionally down?

I had nothing except my NYSC discharge certificate and a strong vision of the future. As the vehicle approached Warri, I made a resolution; I told myself "I will not give up on my future". I resolved to do all it takes within the framework of legality to succeed and fulfill my purpose.

Intrinsically, I had hoped to land a good job as soon as I get to Warri. Two days after my arrival, I decided that it was time to get a job, I launched into the city distributing my Curriculum Vitae (CV), making contact with friends and relatives that are well connected and influential. After several weeks of moving round and meeting people, it suddenly dawned on me that, the job am hoping to get might not come as early as I had hoped. I realised that the list of unemployed graduates was getting longer and longer because I am now on the list.

Wake up! Take This Job!

The list keeps getting longer and longer as higher institutions churn out fresh graduates to add to the already saturated labour market. These graduates go into hibernation for one year, in the name of National Youth Service Corps (NYSC), at the end of the hibernation period, the harsh reality of unemployment stares them in the face like day-break. It is reported that only 10% of graduates of universities and other higher institutions ever get paid employment after the National Service programme.[1]

Undeniably, the unemployment rate in Nigeria is intolerable. But the matter is made worse by the absence of social security and lack of basic amenities. It is even worse when unemployment is concentrated more among the youth. According to the National Bureau of Statistics, Nigeria has a population of over 20.3 million unemployed youths. This is out of a population of about 167 million persons.[2]

With such incredible statistics, one would wonder where in particular we are heading. These are young, energetic men and women, in the prime of their lives.

The youth-age is the most productive age of any man. It is the age of incubation and birthing of ideas that lead to the creation of wealth. This is why it is dangerous for any country to toy with its youth. It is equivalent to aborting the future of that nation.

In my opinion there is no Nigerian household that does not have at least one unemployed University or polytechnic graduate. Thousands of graduates are

---

[1] Reported by Nigerian Tribune of Thursday, 29 March 2012
[2] Reported by This Day Newspaper of, 8th October, 2012

roaming the streets in search of non available jobs. Not that those unemployed graduates do not possess the necessary qualifications but lack indispensable connections in Nigerian context.

From the foregoing, it becomes necessary, as it is advisable before the hammer of unemployment and frustration slams on us, to wake up from our slumber and face the reality of existence by taking proactive measures to secure a brighter future.

I did wake up from my slumber to face life squarely. **Wake up! Take this job!** is an offshoot of the fundamental lessons that I learnt after my NYSC experience.

Wake up! Take this job! provides a paradigm shift from the conventional approach to solving the problem of unemployment. It focuses more on the individual rather than the system. Because the system seem to be irredeemable, but the individual possesses some inherent ability, that if properly harnessed could yield unprecedented result.

According to Zig Ziglar, **"the difference between ordinary and extraordinary is that little extra."** Some people call some jobs "ordinary jobs", but those with foresight see the extra in front of the ordinary; they see the plantation inside the plantain, they see the tree inside the mustard seed.

As you go through the pages of this book, it is my prayer that you will find that extraordinary potential trapped in the so-called ordinary everyday jobs.

In this book, I offer no simplistic solution to a difficult problem. Instead, what you will find is an instrument that will not only inform and reorient you, but is also capable of pushing you out of the complaining zone to the engagement zone; it will open your eyes to see the enormous opportunities that are available to you and show you how to take advantage of them; it will enable you to create a desirable outcome from the undesirable environment that you might find yourself.

I implore you to read this book carefully, drop your pride, hide your certificate, roll up your sleeves and get ready to work.

I trust that God will bless your effort.

Samuel Aghomi
12th April, 2013

Wake up! Take This Job!

CHAPTER

1

"If you are able to understand your perceptions, you can maybe develop strategies to see the target differently-to keep your focus as best as you can"
-Jessica Witt

CHAPTER ONE

BREAKING THE GLASS CEILING!

"We see the world, not as it is, but as we are"
– Talmud

In medicine, there is a marked difference between treating symptoms and curing a medical condition. For instance, if you have a broken or dislocated anklebone, the first symptom of your condition is likely to be a very sharp pain that makes you practically uncomfortable and you will want to have your symptoms (the pain) treated immediately!

However, taking painkillers will not heal your anklebone and true healing is needed before the symptoms can disappear for good. The bone has to be healed first and then the pains will naturally go away.

If you only treat the symptoms (the pain), it will go for a while and almost without doubt will come back again. This will lead you to treat it, again, and again, and again.

If, instead, you look deeper to understand why the problem is occurring, you can fix the underlying systems and processes that caused the problem and the problem will cease to occur.

> For everything we face today, there **is a causative factor (a root cause behind it).**

For everything we face today, there is a causative factor (a root cause behind it). Knowing and understanding the root cause is central to resolving our issues. Once the root has been removed, the effects will be addressed accordingly.

The root cause of most of the challenges we encounter in life is based on our perception: **the way we see the world.**

UNDERSTANDING THE PRINCIPLE OF CAUSE AND EFFECT

"Everything happens for a reason; for every effect there is a specific cause"
-The law of cause and effect

Joblessness is like pain and indeed it is a deep seated pain. It is such an excruciating pain that can adversely affect the totality of the human make-up. The pain of not having a job is not just economical, it is psychological, social, spiritual and physical; it affects the human make up in all ramifications and most importantly, it is an effect of an underlying cause.

The World Health Organisation (WHO) defines Health as a state of complete physical, mental and social well-being and not merely the absence of disease or infirmity[3].

If we go by this definition, we can conclude that a man without a job is not in a state of good health; therefore he is sick. This is very true because I was once in such a state. The debilitating pain that one goes through as a result of joblessness is unquantifiable and unbearable and it cannot be completely relieved until the primary cause is removed. Pain and disease go together, as long as the disease is there, the pain will linger; the disease is the cause and pain is the effect. The disease is

---

[3] Preamble to the Constitution of the World Health Organisation as adopted by the International Health Conference, New York, June, 1946

underneath whereas the pain is on the surface but the moment the disease is cured, the pain will disappear.

But what is the underlying cause of the pain of joblessness?

DIAGNOSING THE CAUSE OF JOBLESSNESS

Make no mistake: joblessness is like any other ailment that is subject to diagnosis. If you make a wrong diagnosis, you will not only treat the wrong thing; but you will also ignore the real problem because you already think you are on track.

The worst thing you can do is to draw wrong conclusions about the cause-and-effect aspects of the problem of joblessness. You do not only have to thoroughly and accurately diagnose what it is that causes the problem but you also need to implement the correct intervention strategies that will solve the problem.

Joblessness is an effect and wrong perception about unemployment and the labour market is the cause. What you think about joblessness is the cause of the pain. The cause is rooted in the mind and embedded in ones thought pattern. If you think wrong thoughts, you will experience wrong outcomes. Wrong perception about anything will always lead to wrong outcome.

SUPER STORIES

Right or wrong perceptions are framed in the mind. But the human mind does not just absorb anything that crosses its path and frame it as a person's perception. It is always first filtered through cultural, historical, psychological and religious sieves before it is absorbed into the mind to form ones point of reference. These 'mind sieves" are called lenses.

Wake up! Take This Job!

An Israeli political theorist Yaron Ezrahi calls these lenses "super stories". A super story, according to Ezrahi consists of a collection of myths, or ideological constructs, tied together by an overall narrative.

According to Ezrahi this super story helps us to explain the world to ourselves to determine what information we will treat as significant and most important, to record our experiences and shape our values. Ezrahi asserted that like any coloured lens, it lets certain rays of light in and blocks out others.[4]

These lenses are the windows through which we see the world. These windows determine whether we see things as black and white or in vibrant colours; they determine what we see and what we refuse to see. These windows are what ultimately determine who wins and who succeeds in life. These windows are summed up in this acronym: WYSIWYG- **W**hat **Y**ou **S**ee **I**s **W**hat **Y**ou **G**et. In simple term, this acronym means that the events of one's life are products of his or her perception.

Perception therefore can be defined as an established mindset or pattern of thinking which a person holds firmly in his or her mind concerning an issue, a situation, an individual or a group of people which affect the outcome of events for the person. Perception is also called point of view.

THE SCREAMING SCREEN

To give us a practical understanding of the concept of perception, if for instance, you go into a television store; you will notice all the televisions on display. On some of them, bright pictures are to be seen, filled with vibrant

---

[4]Thomas L. Friedman (1989) ***From Beirut to Jerusalem*** New York, Double Day Publishing Group.

colours and giving out the sounds of the latest programme. But there are others on display which are only sitting there, their screens dark and silent. Your eyes naturally go to those sets that are on.

There is nothing particularly interesting about a dark television screen. What is the difference? Only one thing: the dark television sets are not connected to power.

Just like those television sets that are powered; that is how a man who views life from the right perspective is powered. Just as you would naturally gravitate towards the TV sets that are switched on, that is how people and things flow toward an individual with a positive perception about life. The screen of a TV set that is powered is screaming for attention, and in most cases, it always catches the attention of customers in the showroom. But the silent ones seldom catch the attention of anyone.

Each of us has the same inherent capacity to attract the good things of this life to ourselves, much like each television set. But how we see life is what determines how much of our inherent capacity is utilized. Instead of sitting back to lament the bad luck and disappointments in life, we could alter our perception, to such extent that our life can begin to advance toward a more profitable end.

I strongly believe that there will not be any significant change in our lives, unless there is first a significant change in our perception. For us to experience new outcome, we must see things differently.

THE FORCE OF PERCEPTION

Perception is one of the strongest forces on earth. Its power can make or break your day, your week, your year and your life. It can destroy your relationship with people, as well as enhance it; it can barricade your way to success as well as bring you to success shore. Your perception can hold you back; when and where others are making progress. Your perception can incapacitate and even incarcerate you; where and when people are celebrating freedom. Your perception is the graveyard of your past, originator of your present situation and the architect of your future experiences. You cannot experience what your eyes and mind cannot see.

The scope of your ambition; the clarity of your vision and the strength of your courage are dependent on what you see in the world that you live in. If you see defeat, it is only a matter of time before defeat will embrace you. But if you see victory amidst defeat, victory will definitely come to you.

THE TRUTH ABOUT FACTS

Perception can either be fact based or faith based. Fact based perception takes centre stage in shaping most of our point of reference because we often form our point of reference from what we perceive with our senses. But faith based perceptions are formed by believing that things can happen contrary to the perception of our senses. I believe that this is the missing link.

> Unemployment is a fact, but joblessness is a mentality.

We have so much framed our mind based on facts, to such an extent that we cannot act based on faith even if such action will be to our benefit.

There are marked differences between facts and faith based perception and it is essential that we know and appreciate where and when to switch our mind one to the others.

Now, facts are the foundation upon which we build things. But faith which stem from the way we see things is the wings with which we fly to our desired destination.
Facts are used for evaluating people and analyzing situations. Faith is used for encouraging people, instilling hope and changing situations.

Facts are derived from human and scientific theory and experimentations. Faith is derived from the infallible word of God from the Holy Scripture.

Facts are what some ordinary people see and get discouraged. Faith is what motivates extraordinary people to see possibilities amidst impossibilities and get fired up to create solutions where problems abound.

This quote from Charles Dickens book "**Hard Times**" underscores the importance of facts.

> *"Now, what I want is Facts. Teach these boys and girls nothing but Facts. Facts alone are wanted in life. Plant nothing else, and root out everything else. You can only form the minds of reasoning animals upon Facts; nothing else will ever be any service to them..."*
> -Charles Dickens

So, it is holding both facts and faith in hand and understanding where each fit in the scheme of things.

For example, "I have to be realistic that I do not have a job (that is fact) and yet at the same time I have to have faith that the present situation can change in my favour and that whatever I lay my hands on to do will prosper (this is faith in action)."

The victorious life, is a life that says "even though I know the facts, yet I am undaunted by it."

Wake up! Take This Job!

Unemployment is a fact, but joblessness is a mentality, it is the product of your perception. The fact that a teeming population of youths are wasting away doing nothing valuable with their precious time is not new, it is as real as day break; in fact it is a global phenomenon. It is just that, in Nigeria the population of such people is very high and nothing is being done by the authorities to address it.

But what you make of life does not depend on the fact that unemployment rate is high; It rather depends first on your perception and secondly, on your response to the way you perceive life to be.

Facts are real, but they are not permanent. Facts can be changed.

"Believe nothing, no matter where you read it, or who said it, no matter if I have said it, unless it agrees with your own reason and your own common sense."
-Buddha

It was once a well established fact that the earth was flat. But that fact has since changed, the earth is actually spherical and not flat.

Also it was once believed that the Great Wall of China is the only manmade structure visible from space.

This fact has been debunked. According to Astronaut Alan Bean:

"The only thing you can see from the moon is a beautiful sphere, mostly white (clouds), some blue (ocean), patches of yellow (deserts), and every once in a while some green vegetation. No man-made object is visible on this scale. In fact, when first leaving earth's orbit and only a few

thousand miles away, no man-made object is visible at that point either."

Get it into your spirit; facts are not permanent, whether they are economical, medical, physical or spiritual. They are subject to changes.

"Men often become what they believe themselves to be. If I believe I cannot do something, it makes me incapable of doing it. But when I believe I can, then I acquire the ability to do it even if I didn't have it in the beginning."
- Mahatma Gandhi

Let me say it again, "Facts are not permanent."

"Man is not the creature of circumstances; circumstances are the creatures of man"
-Benjamin Disraeli

Although facts are not permanent, they are however difficult to change. Established facts can only bow to superior reasoning and a higher logic. Such higher reasoning does not come by focusing on the facts, but by concentrating ones attention on something or someone higher than the source of the established facts.

The fact about unemployment stares at us every day. The official unemployment rate in Nigeria has risen dramatically over the past six years, nearly doubling over the period.

This is reflected in the table below:

Unemployment rate in Nigeria between 2006-2011

Year	2006	2007	2008	2009	2010	2011
Unemployment Rate (%)	12.3	12.7	14.9	19.7	21.4	23.9

Source: Nigeria Bureau of Statistics (NBS)

Unemployment rate can be defined as the number of people actively looking for jobs divided by the labour force. According to the bureau, the figure of unemployed Nigerians in the first half of 2011 was 23.9 per cent, up from 21.4 per cent in 2010 and 19.7 per cent in 2009.

The Statistician-General and Chief Executive Officer, NBS, Dr. Yemi Kale, recently put the number of jobless Nigerians at 20.3 million.[5] The Statistician-General stressed that unemployment was highest among youths aged between 15 and 24, 25 and 44.

You should know that the above data are the official figures. They are likely to be higher.

These facts are real, and they are not likely to change or get better.

But we are not slaves to facts; our lives should not be stagnated by facts and figures. We can choose to act against well established facts and accurate figures and get outstanding results.

"The fact that an opinion has been widely held is no evidence that it is not utterly absurd."-
-Bertrand Russel

Most people who break records are people who acted against well known indisputable facts. If you cannot change the facts surrounding the circumstances of your life, you can change yourself by altering your view of those facts. When your views are positively altered, your reality will definitely change.

"Never accept a fact until it is verified by a theory"

---
[5] *The Nigerian Tribune* Sunday, 10th March 2013

-Sir Arthur Eddington

PERCEPTION AND REALITY

It is said that perception is what defines reality. This is very true, but how can we possibly say that a thing is real or unreal?

If we say that something is real, there are certain characteristics that we ascribe to it. For instance, we say a human being is real, because we can see, feel, hear or smell the person with our senses.

But there are things that are more real, things that we may not see with our eyes, hear with our ears or perceive with our nose; things like love, peace, faith and joy.

> Perception is what defines reality.

They are abstract in nature, yet their presence or absence cannot be denied. How do we know that they exist? We know that they exist because our experience in life has proven the reality of their existence to us.

But, there are people out there who do not believe that love, peace, faith and joy exist. Such people remind me of "Mr. Spock", a character in "STAR TREK" that I read in the book "**12 Habit that holds good people back**"

Spock is a native of the planet Vulcan; he and others of his species appear human in most respects other than their superhuman intellect, pointed ear and inability to either feel emotions themselves or understand them in others.

Spock is courageous (fear being an emotion he could not feel); he is the sort of person you would want by your side if your space ship were hurtling at warp speed into the path of an asteroid belt. He would correct the course in split second without a fluctuation in his pulse rate.

Wake up! Take This Job!

He is also, however, joyless, incapable of love and of no help whatsoever in understanding human nature. His inability to feel is as a result of the environment he lived in before coming to planet earth.[6]

> *If you are jobless, it is your fault*

Such people as Mr. Spock have a hard time recognizing and understanding joy, love, peace, compassion and other emotions in themselves and in others. They see the world and people in particular as though they were looking at an x-ray; all bones without flesh or nervous system. Such people, because of their experiences have successfully repressed their own emotions such that they cannot hear or see what most other people hear and see.

Why have some people become emotionally dead? Their reasons could be traced to things they have experienced. Are they wrong to believe that phenomenon as love, joy and other emotions do not exist? The answer is no. why? Because they see the world from a different perspective.

What you believe to be true is only as true as what you have experienced in this world. It is important to note that how you choose to perceive things is how they come across to you. What you may learn from a situation may be different from what another person will learn from the same situation.

For us to succeed in this world, we should sometime look at things from others point of view. But there are some people who cannot afford to look in a different direction or see things from other's perspective for even

---

[6] Waldrop J. and Butler T. (2000) *The 12 Bad Habit That Hold Good People Back*, New York , Doubleday Random House, Inc.

a split second. Their gaze is permanently fixed; their perspective is like reinforced concrete, practically unmovable and unchangeable.

They cannot hear or see things from others' frame of reference. Such people are often rigid, unbending and adamant because they believe that their point of view is the most valid and superior.

You will discover that a man, who does not believe in love, seldom finds love in this world; A man who does not believe in peace, hardly find peace. But a man, who believes in peace, finds peace even in the midst of crisis.

This principle is also applicable to the mindset of having or not having a job. What you see is what you get. Everything that has happened to you and everything that will happen to you is generated by your perception.

WHY YOU ARE STILL JOBLESS

"Whatever you truly, believe with feeling becomes your reality"

From all that we have said so far, it is crystal clear that if you are jobless, it is your fault. This may be a bitter pill for you to swallow. You may quickly want to take a defensive position by saying that it is the government's responsibility to provide the jobs.

Well if you are taking such position, you are not doing yourself any good because you are playing the blame game and passing the buck in the wrong direction and to the wrong sets of persons.

I know that you are probably thinking that I am not being realistic; that perhaps, I am from a different planet. Well, let me dispel your doubt. I am from

Nigeria, I was educated in Nigeria and I presently live in Warri, Delta State in the heart of the Niger Delta.

You are jobless because you have framed your mind from the prevailing facts about unemployment that are available to you; which has crystallised to form your perception; your perception has incapacitated and deprived you from taking steps that will change your life and consequently, joblessness has become your reality.

"As a man thinketh in his heart so he is."
-Proverbs 23:7

NEW MEANING FROM A DIFFERENT ANGLE

There are different angles to issues of life. You have to look at an issues or a thing from all its different angles before you can say that you know that thing in totality. View things in whole; from the every possible angle and you will get the whole picture.

It is more like the opinion that people have of marriage, some people believe that 1 plus 1 in marriage is equal to 1, others believe that 1 plus 1 equals 2.

Both are correct, what you make out of life depends on your point of view. Every coin has two sides, whether you see tail or head depends on the side of the coin you are looking at.

The meaning of something will change when you look at it differently. You can look at anything differently and it will have a different meaning. When you look at the fact that you do not have a job differently, you will definitely see a new meaning to life.

If you always look at life from one angle, you will always see what you have always seen but if you change your angle of view, what you see will assume a new dimension.

You can reposition your life, by standing on a better platform which provides a vantage point for you to see the future more clearly. As soon as you catch a glimpse of what is to come, your orientation about life will be positively altered.

Have you ever taken time to consider what you can do now that you do not have a job? Have you ever looked around you to see what you can do with your time instead of sitting down at home watching TV from sunrise to sunset? Yes, you can do something worthwhile if you choose to.

CHOOSING TO SEEING THINGS DIFFERENTLY

"When you reach an obstacle, turn it into an opportunity. You have the choice. You can overcome and be a winner, or you can allow it to overcome you and be a loser. The choice is yours and yours alone. Refuse to throw in the towel. Go that extra mile that failures refuse to travel. It is far better to be exhausted from success than to be rested from failure."
- Mary Kay Ash, founder of Mary Kay Cosmetics

Your belief structures determine your perception, which then ultimately determine how you respond to events. It is all a matter of choice; you can choose to examine your beliefs and then choose to change them or refuse to examine them and remain the way you are.

Everything begins with a choice. The choice of changing your perception is by no means an easy one but it is a necessity. It is necessary for you to undo some of

> The meaning of something will change when you look at it differently.

your old beliefs about the labour market, if you want your life to change.

In his classic book: **Awaking the Giant within You**[7] Anthony Robbins said that there are three decisions that control your destiny. According to him these decisions determine what you will do, and ultimately what you will contribute and who you will become.

The three decisions are:
  i. Your decisions about **what you focus on**
  ii. Your decisions about **what things mean to you**
  iii. Your decision about **what to do to create the results you desire**.

These decisions are premised on your perception about life. Your perceptions determine what you focus on; which determine what you consider to be important and the sets of actions you take or refuse to take.

Following the same line of thought, Stephen Covey in his book "***Everyday Greatness***"[8] said that "there are three choices we make every day that determine what becomes of us".

The first of such choice is ***"if we will act upon life or will merely be acted upon. If we will be a driftwood that passively floats with the tides and currents of the day or will we instead take proactive responsibility for determining our actions and destinations?"***

The second choice according to Covey is ***"to what ends or purposes, will our daily choice lead?"***

---

[7] Robbins A. (1991) *Awakening the giant within you,* New York. The Free Press-Simon Schuster, Inc.
[8] Covey, S. (2006) *Everyday Greatness.* Tennessee, Rutledge Hill Press, Thomas Nelson Inc.

And the third choice is ***"will we live our lives in accordance with proven principles, or will we suffer the consequences of not doing so"***

If you carefully observe what these gentlemen are saying, you will see that the event of a man's life stream from his perception.

How do you see life? What do you think about people? What do you expect from situations? What you see is what you get; what you see in the mirror of life; and that is what you ultimately become. The choice is always yours to make.

> ***"The strongest principle of growth lies in human choice"***
> - George Eliot

CHANGE YOUR PERCEPTION, CHANGE YOUR LIFE

Our society is changing. We live in times of rapid change, of global change, a change that probably will have an enormous impact on all of us living on this earth. The Society that we live in is dynamic and not static today.

You and I must either embrace the dynamism inherent in the society we live in or be left behind in the scheme of things. Embracing change is critical to survival in this world.

For instance, if the traditional way of thinking and doing things stands in the way of survival, what are we expected to do? Keep to tradition or embrace novelty?

Wisdom teaches us to follow the pathway that will enhance our survival because if we stick to the old pattern of thinking and doing things, we may face the risk of sliding into oblivion. The easiest way to extinction is refusal to change an obsolete way or method of operation.

Stephen Covey aptly described a man in **"Everyday Greatness"** called a transition person. He said that "a transition person is one who breaks the flow of bad-the negative traditions or harmful practices that get passed from generation to generation, or from situation to situation whether in a family, a workplace, a community, or wherever."

You can be a transition person as Stephen Covey has rightly said. Breaking free from traditions requires that you have a renewed perception which is completely different from the established pattern of thinking.

> **"Problems cannot be solved by the same level of thinking that created them."**
> -Albert Einstein

Fundamentally, perception is deeply entrenched in our consciousness and framed in the innermost part of our mind.

Consciousness is the quality or state of being aware of an external object or something within oneself. It has been defined as: **"subjectivity, awareness, sentience, the ability to experience or to feel, wakefulness, having a sense of selfhood, and the executive control system of the mind"** [9].

Your perception, which flow from your consciousness, is the wings on which the event of your life unfolds. When something is woven into your consciousness, it is only a matter of time before it becomes your reality. Sometimes

---

[9] Farthing G. (1992) *The Psychology of Consciousness*. Prentice Hall.

the gap between reality and consciousness seems to be wide, but it is not.

> *"What you send out mentally over a period of time will return to you in kind, precisely and inevitably"*
> -Norman Vincent Peale

When consciousness and reality seem to be far apart, sooner or later either reality will be made to fit the consciousness or the consciousness made to fit the reality. What this implies is that our predominant thought snowballs into the events of our everyday life.

Changing your perception and seeing things from a different angle is one of the key to survival in this world. Robert Kiyosaki in his book "**Retire young, retire early**[10]" said that: *"Changing one's reality from a middle class or poor reality to a rich reality may be like learning to eat with your left hand after you have spent years eating with your right. While it is not hard to do, and anyone can do it if they persevere, it may not be the easiest thing to do.*

While discussing reality he further said that *"the fastest way to become rich is to be able to change your realities faster."*

SEEKING A DIVORCE FROM JOBLESSNESS

For most Nigerian graduates joblessness has become their reality. Most of them have been having a steady romantic affair with joblessness for a long time as a result of their perception. This romance has infiltrated their entire mental faculty and has significantly influenced their approach to life.

Some have even demanded for a certificate of marriage and since then, the real truth has dawned on them, it

---

[10]Kiyosaki R. (1999) Retire Young, Retire Rich. New York, Warner Books Inc.

Wake up! Take This Job!

has become glaring that an affair with joblessness is actually a marriage with poverty.

Joblessness is now commonplace amongst graduates. It is difficult to talk about being a graduate or discuss with a graduate without talking about joblessness.

It ought not to be so; there should not be any relationship whatsoever between a graduate and joblessness because a graduate has all that is required to either be gainfully employed or to be an employer of labour. The reverse is the case today, because we expect someone or a group of people to come to our aid and free us from the shackles of joblessness.

FIGHTING YOUR OWN BATTLE

What we often fail to realise is that unemployment is a national issue, but joblessness is an individual's problem. You must come to terms with the fact that, getting out of the labour market is your personal fight. It neither your parents, nor the government's fight. It is your fight!

> *Unemployment is a national issue, but joblessness is an individual's problem.*

You are the one that will fight your way out of joblessness. It is you that will break yourself free from the shackles of joblessness. You have to start that fight now!

The assurance in starting this kind of fight is that, you can win! Yes, you can win! Because many have fought and won, your case is not an exception. This book is one of the weapons that can guarantee your victory.

And If in the course of reading this book, you discover that you and unemployment are bedfellows, instead of a marriage certificate, demand for a divorce. You can get that divorce; you can break free from the shackles of joblessness. The first step in the divorce proceedings is a **"change of perception"**.

"Everything you see or hear or experience in any way at all is specific to you. You create a universe by perceiving it, so everything in the universe you perceive is specific to you."
-Douglas Adams

Let us now consider some of the wrong perceptions we might have about employment and the labour market, which are the fundamental reasons why many graduates are sitting at home waiting for jobs.

Until we drop some or all of these perceptions, we might not make headway in our pursuit of a great and better tomorrow.

If you take a careful look at the perceptions below, you might have been held back by at least one or all of them at one time or the other. The good news is that, it is time to break the glass ceiling and you can!

13 WRONG PERCEPTIONS THAT WE HAVE ABOUT EMPLOYMENT

1. Government is responsible for provision of employment for all graduates.

   Right perception: *Government cannot provide job for every graduate. The core responsibility of government is to provide the enabling environment for people to do business. Should the government fail in its responsibility? We should be able to use the available amenities to keep our business alive.*

Wake up! Take This Job!

2. Our well connected and influential family members and friends should pave the way for us to get a good job.

Right perception: *Our family members have given us good education, which is the most important instrument that we need to succeed in this world. With or without their influence and connections, we should be able attain success anywhere.*

3. As soon as I am out of school or NYSC I will be thrown into the labour market where there are no jobs.

Right perception: *There are jobs everywhere. I have to create the kind of job that I desire by starting something with what I have and from where I am.*

4. Because I am from a certain part of the country or ethnic nationality, I must get a job from that area.

Right perception: *That I am from a certain area is not a guarantee that I must get a job from such area. The foreigners who occupy top positions in some companies are not even from Nigeria. I can succeed wherever I find myself.*

5. I must work in an area that is relevant to my qualification.

Right perception: *I can diversify, I can acquire new skills; I can learn a new trade; I can do all sort of things; I can do a job that is not related to the course I studied in the higher institution.*

6. I need a higher degree, certification and qualification to get a better paying job.

Right perception: *I can start with the degree or certificate that I have and later upgrade to a higher degree. I do not necessarily have to wait to get all the higher degrees before I start doing something meaningful with my life.*

7. I will continue to write aptitude test and one day I will get that big job.

Right perception: *I do not have to be travelling everywhere to write aptitude test. Instead, I could engage myself in entrepreneurial pursuit by doing small businesses, while I write aptitude tests.*

8. Since I am a graduate, there are certain jobs that I cannot do.

Right perception: *It is not the job that matters, but the person that does the job, I can bring innovative ideas and creative solutions to those jobs that were considered "not fit" for graduates and make it fit for myself. "na person start shit business for Lagos." In our local Pidgin English, it literally means that somebody started the evacuation of human waste in Lagos, but today it has become a big business.*

9. I rather stay at home, than take a job that is below my qualification.

Right perception: *From the very day I graduate from school or pass out from NYSC I must not spend one day without doing something meaningful that will add value to my life. I rather do a job that is below my qualification, than stay at home doing nothing meaningful with my life. An idle mind is the devil's workshop.*

Wake up! Take This Job!

10. I am too old or too young to do some kind of jobs.

Right perception: *Age is but a number. I am neither too old nor too young to do any job.*

11. I cannot do some kind of jobs because I am a man or woman.

Right perception: *My gender is not a barrier, I can go anywhere and do any job that is morally and legally right.*

12. I cannot get a good job in Nigeria; I must travel abroad for greener pasture.

Right perception: *Abroad is not "above". Nigeria is a blessed country. I can make it here without travelling abroad. The land is green!*

13. An unemployed person is a jobless person.

Right perception: *An unemployed person may not be a jobless person. The fact that you are unemployed by the government or the private sector, does not mean that you cannot be self-employed.*

Some of the above wrong perceptions have kept many intelligent and smart graduates at home doing nothing valuable.

The time has come for you to break free from these limiting perceptions. The time has come for you to alter the course of your life. The time has come for you to break free from the shackles of joblessness.

This is your time! This is your chance for a new start! This may be your finest hour!

You may not be able to change what happens to you, but you always have the power to control what happens

Wake up! Take This Job!

in you and the choice of changing how you respond to whatever happens to you.

You may not be able to change the fact that you have graduated so long ago, without a job; but you can alter the course of your life, by looking at things differently.
At every stage in life, there is always something you can do. There are things you can do today that will resonate positively into your future. Start looking at the event of your life from a different angle and change will come to you.

Let me conclude this chapter with a short story.

CARROT, EGG, AND COFFEE

There is this story about a boy who was so discouraged with failing in school, he told his grandfather he wanted to quit.

His grandfather filled three pots with water and placed each on a high fire. Soon the pots came to a boiling point. In the first, he placed carrots, in the second he placed eggs and the last he placed ground coffee beans. He let them sit and boil, without saying a word. In about twenty minutes he turned off the burners.

He fished the carrots out and placed them in a bowl. He pulled the eggs out and placed them in a bowl. Then he ladled the coffee out into a cup. Turning to the boy, he asked, "Tell me, what you see?" "Carrots, eggs, and coffee," the boy replied.

Then he asked the boy to feel the carrots, which he did and noted that they were soft and mushy. His grandfather then asked him to take an egg and break it. After pulling off the shell, the boy observed the hard-boiled egg. Finally, he asked the boy to sip the coffee. He

Wake up! Take This Job!

smiled as he tasted the coffee with its rich aroma. The boy asked, "I don't understand. What does this mean, if anything?"
His grandfather laughed and explained that each of these objects had faced the same adversity: boiling water, but each had reacted differently. "Which are you?" the grandfather asked. "When adversity knocks on your door, how do you respond?

Are you a carrot that seems strong, but with pain and adversity, becomes soft and loses strength?
Are you the egg that appears not to change but whose heart is hardened?

Or are you the coffee beans that change the hot water, the very circumstance that brings the pain. When the water gets hot, it releases the fragrance and flavor. If you are like the coffee beans, when things are at their worst, your very attitude will change your environment for the better, making it sweet and palatable.

His lesson was that in life when you cannot change the circumstances, change yourself.

LIFE PRINCIPLES FROM CHAPTER ONE

- *For everything we face today, there is a causative factor(a root cause behind it.)*
- *Unemployment is a fact, but joblessness is a mentality.*
- *Perception is what defines reality.*
- *The meaning of something will change when you look at it differently.*
- *Your belief structure determines your perception which then ultimately determines how you respond to events.*
- *The easiest way to extinction is refusal to change an obsolete way or method of operation.*
- *At every stage in life, there is always something you can do.*
- *When something is woven into our consciousness, it is only matter of time before it become our reality.*
- *The strongest principle of growth lies in human choice.*
- *When you cannot change the circumstances, change yourself.*

CHAPTER

2

> "We have always held to the hope, the belief, the conviction that there is a better life, a better world, beyond the horizon"
> -Franklin D. Roosevelt

CHAPTER TWO

NEW DEFINITION, NEW HORIZON

"We all live under the same sky, but we do not all have the same horizon"
- Konrad Adenauer

There is an old adage that says *"**Half of the solution to any problem lies in defining the problem**."* For your perspective to change, you must of a necessity change the platform that you are standing on. This platform more often than not is in the form of a belief system, a long standing tradition and way of doing things. There are belief systems that could be observed in families, others could be noticed in some geographical locations and among different kinds of people; the most challenging are belief systems that are predominant among youths.

It is essential as we try to re-configure our mindset towards getting a job in an economy where the unemployment rate is increasing by the day, that we identify those concept that has been an obstacle to us and redefine them.

Your definition of a concept will affect how you see that concept and how you live your life with respect to the concept.

WHEN DOES A YOUTH BECOME AN ADULT?
Let us start with this question. When does a youth become an adult? If you do a quick survey by asking some persons this question, you will be amazed at the response you will get.

Wake up! Take This Job!

Is it when a youth get his or her driver's license, vote, become financially independent, attain 18 years of age, live on his or her own, have intercourse, get drunk, get arrested, get pregnant or impregnate a girl, get married or graduates from the higher institution?

When does a youth become an adult?

Is there a particular event that marks the transition from youth age to adulthood?

Is there a time in life when a youth automatically becomes an adult?

There is a time and there are events that mark the transition from youth age to adulthood. This transition process is found in different cultures throughout time and in an enormous variety of places.

> Your definition of a concept will affect how you see that concept and how you live your life with respect to the concept.

The process is often called "***Rite of passage***" in most culture and it serves as an opportunity and a blessing, assisting the young person in coping with the inevitable demands and distresses of adult life.

The concept of rites of passage is defined as: "***A ritual event that marks a person's transition from one status to another.***"[11]

There are five major rites of passage that are common in Africa and which are fundamental to human growth, and development.

They are:

---

[11] www.wikipedia.org/wiki/Rite_of_passage

i. **Birth**: from the womb to the world,
ii. **Adulthood**: from Youth age to Adulthood,
iii. **Marriage**: from Singlehood to Matrimony,
iv. **Eldership**: from Adulthood to Eldership
v. **Ancestorship**: from eldership to ancestor

Each of these rites is a key component that is part of most traditional African cultures. These five themes are the thread that links families and villages in traditional Africa and provide the necessary structure for individual growth, development and inclusion in communal activities.

The most significant of these rites is the passage from youth age to adulthood. The age at which this rite is performed and the activity that takes place varies from one culture to the other, the essence is to ensure the shaping of productive and community-oriented responsible adults.

In places where the traditional practice of rite of passage persist; an individual may not be permitted to assume adult life and take up some important responsibilities until after the necessary rites have been performed. Therefore, the person has to wait for his or her time.

From the above line of reasoning, traditionally speaking and by conventional assertion,

> *"A youth may be defined as a young dependant person who is WAITING to transit into adulthood."*

As harmless as this definition may seem, it effect has clogged the wheel of progress for most youth, particularly graduates. You may be wondering how such an ordinary definition can adversely affect the life of an individual.

Be patient and just follow me and you will soon find out how the harm is done.

This definition forms a barrier in the mind, that does not only limit the ability of a young person but has the tendency of undermining the person's potentials and pushing the person into a "cocoon" with a placid mentality of 'let me wait for my turn'.

It is much like the popular saying

"Youths are the leaders of tomorrow"

The implication of this saying is that since youths are the leaders of tomorrow, they should wait for tomorrow before assuming leadership positions.

In line with that they may decide wait patiently for tomorrow to come. Some are already in their 50s and are still waiting to become the leaders they were told they will be in their tomorrow. There is no end to tomorrow because the tomorrow we talked about yesterday is now our today. So why wait for tomorrow that will never come?

Although the traditional rite of passage from youth age to adulthood have been overshadowed by civilization and modernity. However, the mindset of "waiting" still persists in the sub-consciousness of most youth.

The sad news is that many young graduates have unknowingly imbibed this self limiting mindset and are living on the "waiting" side of life. After schooling, they join the waiting list, waiting for government to provide a job for them and expecting the grand ceremony that will announce their entrance into adult life.

MODERN RITE OF PASSAGE

Constitutionally, in Nigeria as well as in many developed country, an individual is considered an adult upon attainment of 18 years of age. At that age the person is responsible for his or her actions but does attainment of 18 years of age confers maturity on an individual?

As we make advances in life and attain certain age, there are different ceremonies that are organized to mark the exit from one level and an entry into another level. Some ceremonies are more grandiose than others.

In modern parlance, the grandest ceremony that commemorates the rite of passage from youth age to adulthood is marriage.

It does not matter how old or how educated a person is, he may not get the kind of respect he desires until he is married and marriage in Nigeria today is a capital intensive project.

Therefore, it could be reasonably accepted that the actual ceremony that marks the transition from youth age to adulthood takes place when an individual secures a high profile corporate job with a fat paycheck. The money earned from such job could provide the means for the person to become a full-fledged adult by being married and then he or she labelled a "big boy" or "big girl".

This is not to say that there are no youth out there with good jobs but for one reason or the other are either not ready or willing to get married. The centre of attention here are those youths whose main hindrance to cross from youth age to adulthood is their inability to get a job.

WAIT NO MORE!

Wake up! Take This Job!

> *"Change will not come if we wait for some other person or some other time. We are the ones we have been waiting for. We are the change that we seek."*
> -Barack Obama

I am yet to comprehend why most graduates enter into hibernation after graduation. By hibernation I mean a world of inactivity, un-productivity and dependency; a world of idleness and stagnation and a world of waiting for the so-called high-profile–corporate-job, instead of being engaged doing something worthwhile.

Many have joined the long and ever increasing list of those that are waiting for the government or the private sector to provide jobs for them. They are waiting for the job that will provide the means for them to attain adulthood. While they are waiting, the world is moving on. This long wait is unnecessary; it is a sheer waste of precious time and an impediment to the realization and release of valuable potentials.

The most pathetic youth in Nigeria today, is that youth that will sit at home doing nothing other than waiting and expecting to land a high profile corporate job, just because he or she has gone to a citadel of learning and has earned a degree.

In contrast, the smartest youths in Nigeria are those who refuse to wait for a job either from the government or the private sector and are taking the bull by the horn by using their education to earn a living.

It is my sincere desire that you would be enlisted among the few smart Nigerian youths. These few youths have discovered a new definition to the concept of youth, and they are advancing with it.

It is a definition that can catapult you from the waiting list and land you among the league of entrepreneur. This definition was instrumental to my resolution not to wait for the unavailable jobs instead to take advantage of the opportunities that are around me. It is this definition that I am advocating.

To redefine the concept of youth, I adopted the definition that was used in the document ***"Youth – Investing and Empowering"***.[12] It defines youth as ***"the passage from a dependant childhood to an Independent adulthood"***.

This definition is a deviation from the status quo. It shows that the category of "youth" does not correspond to a simple quantitative dimension defined by age or educational attainment. It emphasizes the fact that a youth irrespective of his or her age is one who has moved from a dependent child to an independent adult.

The "passage" to independence involves series of transformative processes. Just as there are different stages in life, so also there are different stages in the process of attaining adulthood, until the youth finally undergoes complete metamorphosis and attains all-round independence.

The time at which these changes occurs in the past was determined by culture but in our world today the changes that take place in the transformation of a youth to an adult is no longer determine by culture as it was in the time of our fore fathers or by education as is obtainable in some environments today. Only one

---

[12] EU Youth Report, SEC (2009) Youth - Investing and empowering", 549 final.
http://www.un.org/esa/socdev/youthemployment/yenpr.doc

person can determine when the changes should happen: **You, the individual.**

> *"Maturity includes the recognition that no one is going to see anything in us that we don't see in ourselves. Stop waiting for a producer. Produce yourself."*
> -Marianne Williamson

Only you can decide when to take your destiny into your hands. Only you can decide when you want or wish to enter into adulthood.

RESPONSIBILITY AND ADULTHOOD

Adulthood has more to do with a person's mindset and his or her ability to take up responsibilities, than the person's age and educational attainment. Adulthood is a declaration of independence; the attainment of full maturity and a cessation of childhood and its tendencies.

That means as long as you are dependent and still carry the paraphernalia of a child; you are still a child. As long as someone else is responsible for you, you still fall into the categorization called "childhood", whether you are sixteen or thirty six years old.

The Holy writ says *"…when I was a child, I spoke and thought and reasoned as a child does. But when I became a man my thought grew far beyond those of childhood, and now I have put away the childish things."*
-1 Corinthians 13:11 (TLB)

We can readily conclude from the above scripture that adulthood is a thing of the mind. It is rooted in the thought pattern of the individual. It is possible for an individual to have gone through the citadel of higher learning and attained a certain age that is accepted by society as the age of maturity and still carry the mentality and reasoning capacity of a child.

On the contrary, there are lots of young folks out there who may not be schooled and may not have attained the age prescribed by society for adulthood, yet they are doing things that a responsible adult would do.

It therefore implies that adulthood is not a function of age, class or educational attainment; it is the ability to respond to responsibilities. That is why an adult who is responding to responsibilities is often called a responsible person.

REDEFINING INDEPENDENCE

Another concept that we need to redefine is independence.

It is defined as Freedom *from the control or influence of another or others*.

The Oxford Advanced Learner's Dictionary 7th Edition renders the term to mean:

> *"The freedom to organize your own life and make your own decisions without needing the help of other people."*

It is a state of being spiritually, physically, emotionally and economically free. It is a state of being free in thought as well as in action. This freedom is holistic. You are not totally free if you are economically dependent.

Economic freedom is the best form of freedom, no matter how much freedom you have: freedom of speech, worship, movement, name it; it does not really matter if you are not free financially. In fact, if you are not free financially, you may not to enjoy the other forms of freedom.

> *"True individual freedom cannot exist without economic security and independence. People who are hungry and out of a job are the stuff of which dictatorships are made"*
> -Franklin D. Roosevelt

Financial freedom is a major driving force behind almost everything that we do on earth. Financial independence is a major goal of every human. As a youth, I believe that financial freedom is or should be one of your major goals in life because your independence is not complete if your pocket is empty.

> *"Infuse your life with action. Don't wait for it to happen. Make it happen. Make your own future. Make your own hope. Make your own love. And whatever your beliefs, honor your creator, not by passively waiting for grace to come down from upon high, but by doing what you can to make grace happen... yourself, right now, right down here on Earth."*
> -Bradley Whitford

I bring this chapter to a close with this quote from one of my mentors.

> *"Education is preparing you to be independent socioeconomically"*
> -E.E. Ukeredi

LIFE PRINCIPLES FROM CHAPTER TWO

- *Half of the solution to any problem lies in defining the problem.*
- *Your definition of a concept will affect how you see that concept and how you live your life with respect to the concept.*
- *You are not totally free, if you are economically dependent.*
- *Freedom is the aspiration of every creature.*
- *Financial freedom is a major driving force behind almost everything that we do on earth.*
- *Adulthood is a declaration of independence; the attainment of full maturity and a cessation of childhood and its tendencies.*
- *Adulthood is not a function of age, class or educational attainment; it is the ability to respond to responsibilities.*
- *You should become the change you seek in the world.*

CHAPTER

3

"The only freedom which deserves the name is that of pursuing our own good, in our own way, so long as we do not attempt to deprive others of theirs, or impede their efforts to obtain it."
–John Stuart Mill

CHAPTER THREE

THE ROAD TO INDEPENDENCE

"Freedom is nothing but a chance to be better."
-Albert Camus

Independence Day celebration is an event that is always marked with pomp and pageantry. But the attainment of independence is a long process; it is often fought for by people with brain and brawn, by men and women who are tired of living in servitude and as a consequence willing to risk all they have to attain freedom. Some have attained independence by pulling the trigger and firing bullets, others by putting pen to paper. Either way, as sweet as freedom is, it is not easily attained.

Let us consider our beloved country Nigeria for instance, more than five decades ago we gained our independence from the colonial power of Great Britain. Every October 1st we remind ourselves that we are an independent Nation.

Our nation's independence is a source of pride for every Nigerian because it marks the day when our nation became the master of its own destiny – free from outside control, so to speak. But are we truly free?

"To be independent is the business of a few only; it is the privilege of the strong"
-Friedrich Nietzsche

THE QUEST FOR FREEDOM

Freedom is the aspiration of every creature. The bird in the cage seeks freedom; the lion in the zoo desires the beauty of the jungle; the fish that is entangled in a net yearn for freedom. Every creature that is in bondage seeks freedom. A man within the wall of a prison seeks for freedom. Freedom is the desire of every man.

Imagine the day when the definition of "independent" will apply to you – the day you will stop depending on another for your livelihood or subsistence.

Gaining true independence for an individual as well as for a country is a long process that requires a lot of work and only few are willing to go through it.

> Freedom is the aspiration of every creature.

Only few are willing to pay the prize for freedom.

There are some salient facts about freedom that I have discovered, let me share them with you.

- Freedom is not free; it must be fought for or paid for.
- For every freedom you are presently enjoying, someone has either paid for it or fought for it.
- Freedom is not permanent, it must be deliberately and constantly protected, preserved, and effectively transfered to the next generation
- Freedom is not absolute; it is dependent on the availability of some factors. Putting the necessary freedom-dependent-factors in place is as important as freedom itself.
- The amount of freedom you enjoy is determined by the quantity and quality of education and awareness that you have.

THE ROUGH AND RUGGED ROAD TO INDEPENDENCE

"In the truest sense, freedom cannot be bestowed; it must be achieved"
-Franklin D. Roosevelt

The process of attaining an independent adulthood started when our parents first enrolled us in kindergarten (for those who were privileged to attend one), for others it was straight from the home to "*Akara School*"[13] and then to primary and secondary school.

The struggle continued till we eventually gained admission into the University or any of the citadels of higher learning to study a course that may or may not be our choice.

For four years or more we battle to get the best of grades. Several hours of sleepless night were invested to make the most of the schooling experience. The climax of all our effort is to graduate with outstanding result.

AFTER GRADUATION WHAT NEXT?

Now schooling and NYSC are over, your dream has come true! You have that degree and discharge certificate that you have long laboured for and you are ready to take the world by storm! Only one thing stands between you, your professional success and financial freedom. You do not have a job.

So now what are you going to do?

The above question is a question that can make you edgy. Particularly when you are confronted with a

---

[13] ***Akara School*** is a term used in Pidgin language to mean a local or substandard nursery school, where a child of low income parents attends.

situation that is beyond your control. One of such situation is landing a job after graduation.

LABOUR MARKET: THE STRANGE, BUT REAL WORLD

After graduation and completion of NYSC, the stressful process of going out into the real world to find a job begins. With no roadmaps, no clearly defined instructions, and no counsellor to guide you through the many difficulties and challenges of a first-time job search, you are left alone to figure out how best to enter a world about which you know relatively little.

Equipped with a good result; you expect your certificate to land you a high profile job in a great firm that pays handsomely.

With high hopes and great expectations you step into the labour market and with confidence in your stride you begin to transit from one company to the other.

Often, you might begin a massive online Curriculum Vitae (CV) distribution and wait for employers of labour to call, or for an SMS to be sent to your mobile phones or for an email to be sent to your email box.

Eagerly, but patiently you wait, anticipating calls. Within weeks your high hopes are deflated and your enthusiasm is dampened. No calls, no SMS and no emails. The little money you managed to save during the NYSC year has gone down the drain for transportation from one place to the other to write aptitude test and attend interviews with potential employers.

Having done all that you know how to do without any tangible result and with your bank account empty. You end up broke and still without a job.
And that question pop-up again.

So now what are you going to do?

THE DILEMMA OF A NIGERIAN GRADUATE

"A hungry man is not a free man"
-Adlai E. Stevenson

Life has never been easy for any fresh graduate, except for the privileged few, whose parents or relations charted a path for them and ensured that they get placement in some of the big companies and government parastatals immediately after graduation.

A larger population is thrown into the labour market, without the hope of landing a decent job.

As a young graduate that is fresh from the University, when you are thrown into the labour market, there is no soft landing for you, because being a graduate does not immunise you from the harsh economic reality of today.

In fact being a graduate puts you in a more difficult situation than your age mates who were not schooled, because your unschooled friends can easily pick up odd jobs, but with your certificate, it is very difficult to do the undesirable jobs.

With all the knowledge you acquired, one, two, three, four, five years down the line with no job and no hope of getting one, instead of being independent, you become more dependent. Frustration may set in and you might begin to contemplate other alternatives.

THE OPTIONS THAT ARE OPENED TO YOU

What are the likely alternatives for you as a fresh graduate? After graduation you have three possible options:

i. Struggle to get a job,

Wake up! Take This Job!

ii. Get back to school for your Post Graduate Diploma, MBA, Master's or any higher degree
iii. Start up your own business.

With the Nigerian economy being what it is today, many graduates are choosing to go back to school for Post Graduate Studies, the reason being: Finding a job is nearly impossible given the high unemployment rate in the country and the discrimination of young graduates by employers of labour on the ground of lack of experience.

Beside these, most professional jobs include the discouraging words "Bachelors degree required, Masters Degree preferred."

> *"Obtaining your Master's degree is not a guarantee for a good job."*

Most graduates are actually in pursuit of Post Graduate Degrees because they believe that such higher qualification can give them the competitive edge when they are sourcing for a job.

But, obtaining a higher degree is neither a guarantee for a good job, nor a visa that will catapult you out of the labour market.

Strangely enough, your master's or higher degree may even be a barrier to you getting some kind of jobs meant for degree holders; you might be labelled "over qualified".

To buttress the fact that a higher degree is not a visa to securing a good job; there was this headline on the front page of Vanguard of 5th November 2012, which reads as follows:

6 PhD, 704 Masters Holders among applicants for driver's job in Dangote.

The detail of the news reads:

> "**The ugly unemployment statistics of Nigeria has been highlighted by the number of applications from higher degree and first degree holders who sought employment as drivers in Dangote Group. The staggering figure stands at 13,000. Of the 13,000 applications received by the Dangote Group for the Graduate Executive Truck Drivers there were <u>6 PhD, 704 Masters and 8,460 bachelor degree holder.</u> The company only needed 100 drivers.**"

In spite of the above discouraging news, getting your Masters degree, Post Graduate Diploma (PGD) or any other higher qualification is not a bad idea, but the process of getting it could make you a dependant once again, particularly if you are studying on full time basis.

Also, it becomes more challenging if you are from a family that is not too financially buoyant. The question then is who pays for your tuition, accommodation and other expenses? If you cannot answer this question with some level of assurance, you need to have a rethink about going back to school.

My humble submission on the subject of getting a higher degree is that, you should concentrate your attention on getting something with what you already have. Use the degree or the qualification that you have to get your life started.

Wake up! Take This Job!

If you accept my recommendation, then you are stuck with the first and third options: Struggle to get a job or start up your own business.

Most graduates will choose the first option, because it seems to be the most logical path to follow. However, there is a handful that chooses the third option; we shall discuss more on the importance of this choice in chapter eight.

For now, let us focus our attention on those who choose the first option.
So you decide to take your chances, step out of the house and search for a job.

PLENTY OF WORK AMIDST SCARCITY OF JOBS

"We're a society that knows how to apply for a job. The challenge for employment seekers today is to become proficient at finding work. That's a much more complicated process than applying for a job."
-Anonymous

Is there really a job out there for you?

I want you to really think about it, is there really a job out there for you?

If your answer is yes, the next question is as important as the first.

What kind of job is out there?

Unlike the wrong perception that many graduates have in their mind, that there are no jobs. The truth is that there are jobs out there.

As I said in the opening chapter of this book, Unemployment is real, but joblessness is a mentality. If you think there are no jobs out there, then there are no jobs; if you think you are jobless then, you are jobless. I

Wake up! Take This Job!

have left the NYSC for close to three years, I am yet to spend one day without working.

> *If you think there are no jobs out there, then there are no jobs; if you think you are jobless then, you are jobless.*

There are lots of jobs out there for different people; you might not see or get the kind of job that you have always desired. The truth is that there are jobs out there for people who really want to work. What you need is humility. Humility can take you anywhere.

If there are lots of jobs out there, why are there many graduates without a job? The answers is simple: most graduates focus their job search on high profile, high waged public and private sector positions and as a result they are willing to wait in line for such jobs and remain jobless for a long time.

The truth is that hunting for jobs in the public and private sector is time-consuming, with little or no guarantee of landing one. But the time you put into seeking such traditional employment and travelling the length and breadth of the country; writing aptitude test and attending interviews, could be spent in getting creative in your approach, you could learn how to make money through entrepreneurial pursuit until you actually land your desired job.

While you are waiting to land that high profile job, the reality is that in the meantime, you still have to take care of yourself and pay your bills.

The job you are searching for might not come when you expect it. You always have a choice, it is either you make use of your brain and make some gains or you get drained in your search for the conventional jobs.

WHY DO YOU NEED A JOB, ANYWAY?

Do you need a job? Why do you need a job? Such question could be viewed as unnecessary, but it is not. A blind man once met Jesus Christ, and Jesus asked him what he wanted. He was obviously blind; Jesus wanted to know if he really knew what he wanted.

Why do you want a job? Of what benefit will a job be to you? You must know why you want whatever you want. If you need a job, you must know why you need it. No assumption.

You must be sure of why you need what you need. Knowing the reason why you need a job could be enough motivation to propel you to get one.

But, what is work?

Work is not easy to define. One person's idea of work can be another person's idea of leisure. Something that you dislike doing at work, you might quite enjoy in a leisure setting.

> A man without money is as defenseless as a city without walls. He cannot have access to the basic necessity of life.

Most dictionary definitions of the word 'work' say that work activity is directed at a specific purpose, and involves mental or physical effort to earn a living.

People usually work to get the things that they need to live the life that they desire. The most basic human needs are food, clothing and shelter. People need to earn money to take care of these basic necessities of life.

MY MONEY AND MY WORK

The primary reason why people need jobs is to earn money. There could be other secondary reasons. But the bottom line is money, because as the scripture rightly said "**Money answereth all things** and **money is a defense**." A man without money is as defenseless as an ancient city without walls. He will be exposed to external aggressions. He cannot have access to the basic necessities of life. He will be disrespected by people around him.

Money gives you confidence and attracts respect to you. Money gives you a voice, even when you do not have anything to say. Without money, you may be loaded with stuffs and not be given the platform to speak. Money makes people to think that an individual is wise, even if he is foolish.

If money is the main motivation behind work, it is also true that you do not necessarily need to go to school to know how to make money. Schooling can enhance your money making ability. But it is not a prerequisite to making or earning money.

There are many stark illiterates that are millionaires. They cannot even spell their names, yet they make millions.

If the primary purpose of work is to earn money. It means that any work that can produce money has fulfilled its purpose.

"Perfect freedom is reserved for the man who lives by his own work and in that work does what he wants to do"
-Robin G. Collingwood

BREAKING FREE FROM THE PACK

I guess you have seen a herd of cattle. They move together and eventually end up together. I discovered that most students and even graduates think alike; this is irrespective of the higher institution they attend. I call it: **The good life after graduation mentality**.

The thought pattern is somewhat like this:
- Make good grades;
- Do my youth service (NYSC) in the city with a reputable firm;
- Be retained in the firm or land a high profile corporate job after NYSC;
- Earn big money and
- Live happily ever after

As a graduate, I guess you had that kind of thinking or something close. I had it too.

The truth is that life seldom plays out like that. Such thinking might just be a mirage. In fact, the first sign that all might not end up as you probably had thought, is when you get your letter of posting to your place of primary assignment at the NYSC camp and realised that you have been posted to one interior village that is several kilometers from the city to serve as a classroom teacher, with poor accommodation; no electricity; no portable water and no telecommunication network. You will begin to wonder if all your lofty dreams will ever materialise.

There is however an exception for those who had parents or relatives that are well connected. The story is different. Their influential and well connected parents or close relatives will work it out for them, such that immediately after graduation, everything is planned out.

The State where they will do their youth service, the local government, and the company, everything is well prearranged. And immediately after NYSC, the job is waiting.

Another exception is the few that by a dint of God's grace were able to land a decent job immediately after graduation or NYSC.

However, a large population of graduates does not fall into the two exceptions above, although they had the **"good life after graduation mentality"**, but thinking or fantasizing alone will not make it happen. The line of thinking expressed above, might just end in the archive of the mind and not see the light of day, if nothing is done.

Such thinking is good, but it does not always work out that way. If you will ever get what you desire in life, you need to modify your thinking pattern. You need a change, you need to shift your thinking from the narrow world of **'searching for a job'** to the limitless world of creating one for yourself.

It is funny that when people reach a certain age, such as after graduating from the University, they assume it is time to go out and get that high profile job. But like many things the masses do, just because everyone does it, does not mean it is a good idea.

"Patterning your life around other's opinions is nothing more than slavery"
- Lawana Blackwell

In fact, if you are reasonably intelligent, searching endlessly for a job is one of the worst things you can do to yourself. Such endless search could lead to frustration and lose of confidence.

"If you want to retire young and retire rich, you need to think about how to be less employable and not more employable."
-Robert Kiyosaki

DECLARING YOUR OWN INDEPENDENCE

Your parents have given you an education; it is time for you to become independent. Nobody is going to give you independence; you have to get it for yourself. For you to attain your own independence, you must observe the following:

Move out of your parent's house: For you to become independent, you must have a territory - a place of your own. You must have a domain where you can exact your independence. You cannot exert your independence within the four walls of your parent's house.

For you to really start living, you must move out of your parent's house. This is a difficult step on the journey to independent living; however, it is a crucial and critical one that you must take. And you should take it now!

As long as someone else is paying your bills, you are likely not to put your brain to work. You must start living on your own and doing things by yourself.

Some of us are strongly tied to the apron string of our parents, because we are afraid to step out and live on our own. This fear is unnecessary. You should decide not to stay with your parents after graduation Or NYSC.

There are some youths that are above thirty years old and still living in the comfort of their parent's house. This is bad for the individual as well as the family.

As long as you are living with your parents, you will never learn how to work hard or fight your own battles.

Start on a career path. To be completely free, you must be financially free. You become financially free by engaging in something worthwhile that generate income.

You can start by experimenting with different careers and find the one that you enjoy most. If money makes you happy, be an investment banker or start a small business. If you love children, be a teacher. If you like being an expert, then strive to become a consultant in a particular field. If you enjoy talking to people, be a salesperson, motivational speaker or go into the services industry. If knowing how things work is more your passion, try engineering. Working in a career that you enjoy is a part of becoming a mature person.

By all means attach yourself to something that will put money in your pocket and also give you some level of satisfaction.

Maintain a single stable relationship: Relationship is critical to freedom. The idea that some people have of independence is a guy or a lady that keeps multiple relationships without commitment. This is very wrong. Keeping multiple relationships drains you of time, energy and financial resources.

An individual who maintains multiple affairs tends to be emotionally dislocated and mentally unbalance. He or she is often ambivalent, doubt-minded and confused.

The scripture says that:
[For being as he is] a man of two minds (hesitating, dubious, irresolute), [he is] unstable and unreliable and uncertain about everything [he thinks, feels, decides].
(AMP)
- James 1:8

To attain true independence, you should maintain a single and stable relationship that will dovetail to marriage.

As I begin to windup this chapter, I want you to know that whatever you become is your making. Your freedom is up to you. You could continue to explain the number of interviews you have attended and narrating the number of aptitude test you have written without success to anyone or everyone who cares to listen. Or you could spring up surprises by taking the unexpected path of creating a job for yourself and blazing a trail for others to follow. The choice is completely yours to make.

> *"If you do not like something, change it. If you can't change it, change your attitude. Do not complain."*
> –Maya Angelou

I closed this chapter with this short story:

THE PLEASURE OF FREEDOM

Once in a jungle a beautiful golden bird had made her home on a tree. When she sang, shiny pearls fell from her open beak.

One day a bird catcher came to the jungle. Soon he spread a net and the poor golden bird was caught in it. The bird catcher took the bird home and kept it in a silver cage and fed it well. But the sad bird did not sing at all and the hunter never got any pearls.

The bird catcher sold the caged bird to a merchant. The merchant gave the golden bird to the king as a gift. The king thought, "Hmm ... that's a nice bird. I will give it to the princess to play with."

So the king gave the caged bird to the princess.

She was a beautiful girl with a kind heart.

She at once freed the golden bird. The pleasure of freedom made the golden bird sing aloud and soon a shower of pearls fell in the room of princess.

Wake up! Take This Job!

The golden bird came to meet the princess everyday and sang for her. [14]

The lesson here is that freedom brings out your potentials to life.

Follow me in the next chapter as we explore some reasons why you need to alter your attitude, so that you can get to the altitude.

---

[14]Retrieved from www.english-for-students.com/pleasure-of -freedom

LIFE PRINCIPLES FROM CHAPTER THREE

- *Freedom is not free; it must be fought for or paid for.*
- *For every freedom you are presently enjoying, someone has either paid for it or fought for it.*
- *Freedom is not permanent, it must be protected, preserve and transfer to the next generation*
- *Freedom is not absolute; it is dependent on the availability of some factors. Putting the freedom-dependent-factors in place is as important as freedom itself.*
- *The amount of freedom you enjoy is determined by the quantity and quality of education and awareness you have.*
- *Schooling can enhance your money making ability. But it is not a prerequisite to making or earning money.*
- *As long as you are living with your parents, you will never learn how to work hard or fight your own battles.*
- *Your personal freedom ends at the tipoff your nose.*
- *Freedom always goes with responsibility*

CHAPTER

4

"Negativity is very nasty and contagious disease. Remove yourself from all negative people, situations, and things. Choosing to be positive will help you maintain a better attitude, better health, and mindset"

-Jefroy Hanson

CHAPTER FOUR

ADJUST YOUR ATTITUDE

"Your perception is mirrored in your attitude to life."
-Samuel Aghomi

In his book, *The Winning Attitude*[15], John C. Maxwell defines attitude as an inward feeling expressed by behaviour. That is one of the reasons an attitude can be seen without a word being said. He is of the opinion that of all the things we wear, our expression is the most important. In his expanded definition of the term attitude, he gives the following on the subject:

Attitude ...

It is the "advanced man" of our true selves.
Its roots are inward but its fruit is outward.
It is our best friend or our worst enemy.
It is more honest and more consistent than our words.
It is an outward look based on past experiences.
It is a thing that draws people to us or repels them.
It is never content until it is expressed.
It is the librarian of our past.
It is the speaker of our present.
It is the prophet of our future.

---

[15] Maxwell, John C. (1993), *The Winning Attitude*. Nashville, Tennessee: Thomas Nelson, Inc.

Wake up! Take This Job!

Dr. Alan Zimmerman in his book *Pivot: How One Turn in Attitude can Lead to Success*[16], has noticed that attitude makes a huge difference in determining a person's level of success in life. He made this assumption following an extensive observation after speaking for various organisations for more than twenty years.

In essence, he argues that attitude seems to make a bigger difference than age, sex, race, education, circumstance, or any other factor. Two people can have the same background and face the same situations, but experience very different outcomes. It is all about attitude, he asserts.

Zimmerman maintains that attitudes have a definite biochemical effect on the body. An attitude of defeat or panic applies pressure on the blood vessels and has a debilitating effect on the entire endocrine system. On the contrary, an attitude of confidence and determination activates compassionate, therapeutic secretion in the brain.

> *For anyone who desires a positive attitude, there is going to be a need to be committed enough to cultivate it.*

He strikes the difference between negative attitude and positive attitude as follows:

- Whereas the person with a positive attitude (the winner) is always a part of the answer, the loser (with a negative attitude) is always part of the problem.

---

[16] Zimmerman, Alan R. (2006) *Pivot: How One Turn In Attitude Can Lead To Success.* Austin Texas: Peak Performance Publishers.

- Whereas the person with a positive attitude (the winner) always has a programme, the loser (with a negative attitude) always has an excuse.

- Whereas the person with a positive attitude (the winner) says, "Let me help you", the loser (with a negative attitude) says "that is not my job".

- Whereas the person with a positive attitude (the winner) sees an answer for every problem, the loser (with a negative attitude) always sees the problem in every answer.

- Whereas the person with a positive attitude (the winner) says, "It may be difficult but it is possible," the loser (with a negative attitude) says, "It may be possible but it is too difficult."

THE SUCCESS BLOCKER

Dr. Zimmerman asserts that the end result of nursing negativity is that we wind up with millions of people who never come close to using their full potential. Worse still, we end with millions of people who spend more time tearing themselves down than they do building themselves up. He believes that incidentally very few people are fully aware of the negativity in their lives and most of them have no idea how much damage they do to themselves by nursing the negative attitude. Owing to the fact that negativity comes in different forms, he argues that most people do not realise that they may be their own worst enemies.

Wake up! Take This Job!

Dr. Zimmerman suggests that, excuses, fear, pain avoidance, bad habits, and lack of goals, among others, are some of the ways through which negativity may have infiltrated one's life or may be getting in the way of one's success.

> *An attitude of defeat or panic applies pressure on the blood vessels and has a debilitating effect on the entire endocrine system.*

POSSIBLE CAUSES OF NEGATIVE ATTITUDE

i. Excuses

Although one's excuses may sound perfectly reasonable or even justifiable, Dr. Zimmerman maintains that making excuses is one of the ways through which one may be sabotaging himself or herself unknowingly.

According to Zimmerman, someone who is good at making excuses is rarely good for anything else. He argues that the difference between winners and losers is the way they view their circumstances. Whereas losers use their circumstances as an *excuse* to give up, winners use their circumstances as a *reason* to get going and that's one of the reasons why some people become winners while others become losers in the same situation.

He proceeds further by giving an account of Walt Disney, a man who decided to use his circumstances as a reason to work harder instead of excusing himself. From a tender age, Walt Disney was a dreamer who loved to dwell in the world of fantasy, entertainment, and cartoon. But his success as a cartoonist did not come easy; it took determination.

Wake up! Take This Job!

In his first attempt, Walt approached a Kansas City newspaper with his drawings and the editor responded, "These won't do. If I were you, I'd give up this work. From these sketches, it is obvious your talent lies elsewhere."

> *If you have no picture of the future, there is no way you can have a positive attitude toward life.*

Nevertheless, despite the editor's negative consideration, Walt was determined to pursue his strong desire of becoming a cartoonist. Walt experienced rejection after rejection as he tried other newspapers as well. With perseverance, he kept knocking on doors until he eventually was offered the job of drawing publicity material for churches.

Thereafter, Walt embarked on a studio search and all he could find was an old mouse-infested garage. However, while in that garage studio Walt continued to draw his cartoons and write. It was from that determined humble beginning that he eventually became world famous.

Dr. Zimmerman suggests that under the circumstances, Walt could have developed a negative attitude as he had the opportunity of easily making the excuses for not pursuing his dream to be a cartoonist. Nevertheless, Walt understood that someone who is good at making excuses is rarely good at anything else.

ii. Fear

According to Dr. Zimmerman, fear is another possible avenue through which someone may yield to negative attitudes. The fear of failure can stop you from achieving your goal.

Author John Gardner once said,
"One of the reasons mature people stop learning is that they become less and less willing to risk failure."

Zimmerman points out that although some of the fears are normal and healthy because they point out the dangers of life thereby protecting someone from harm, a lot of people are burdened with abnormal fear that prevents them from living a full life or having a productive career.

He also argues that abnormal fear can inhibit action as it hinders people from trying. Instead of making progress, abnormal fear encourages people to make excuses.

He maintains that sometimes people can get a glimpse of new opportunities and approaches in the area of, communication or management, but cannot dare to give it a try because they are stifled by the fear of failure.

As Shakespeare once wrote,
"Our fears do make us fail to try and gain the heights that are possible for us."

Dr. Zimmerman suggests that the choice is yours; either allow fear to dominate and ruin your life or you can choose to dominate and reign over your fears.

iii.   Avoiding Pain
According to Dr. Zimmerman, an increasing desire to keep away from pain can be another avenue through which negative attitudes can find their way into one's life. He argues that by someone thinking that a particular goal would be too hard to attain, he is making a "rational" attempt to avoid pain.

Someone may not be willing to do what it takes to achieve a given goal simply because it may hurt. He agrees with the saying, "no pain, no gain." Since most people do not want to experience any pain, they would rather give up on their goals.

Dr. Zimmerman said, "People often refuse to do the things they have to do to get the results they want. Once again, negative attitudes block success."

He asserts that whereas some people get stuck in their old ways by refusing to do what needs to be done in order to achieve a given goal or number of goals, there are those who put things off instead of doing them immediately. While those with a negative mentality think it is too hard, people with a positive attitude understand that things worth having are worth the effort.

Taking physical fitness as an example, he suggests that at times you may have to do things you do not want to do, for instance, working out day after day whether you like it or not in order for you to build the body that you desire. He claims that whereas many people know they should change, and they are aware that those changes will bring about something far better than what they presently have, they are not willing to go through the pain and discomfort that is needed to get there. At times they keep on postponing doing the things they hate in order to create those things they love.

iv. Lack of Goals

According to Dr. Zimmerman, negative attitudes can hinder someone from setting goals. He views this as being disastrous because there is a clear connection between setting goals and higher achievement. By writing down goals, it helps give one's mind something to focus on which in turn enables the mind to go to work in achieving them.

Dr. Zimmerman maintains that if someone has a negative attitude, it has a tendency of showing up in that person's lack of goals. He argues also that one's lack of goals will lead to a lack of discipline as well. Concerning goals, he gives an example of how a goal can lead a person to set his or her alarm for 5 a.m., and motivates him or her to get out of bed and into the gym for morning exercise purposes.

According to Zimmerman, lack of goals leads to lack of wisdom. Hence those who lack goals will spend most of their time on activities that are tension relieving other than goal achieving.

He suggests that if you want to be wildly successful, it is imperative to get rid of negative attitudes and engage in setting goals. In the light of negative attitudes, he attests to the fact that most people do fail in life because they do not think the thoughts and do the things that will change their circumstances.

UNDERSTANDING THE POWER OF ATTITUDE

In his book *Attitude Is Everything*[17], Keith Harrell emphasizes the fact that it is imperative to manage and control the quality of one's life through the influence of a positive attitude.

According to Harrell, attitude can be viewed as the foundation and support of everything we do; a key

---

[17] Harrell, Keith (2003), *The attitude is everything workbook: Strategies and tools for developing personal and professional success.* New York: HarperCollins Publishers Inc.

element in the process of controlling one's destiny and attaining mastery in one's personal and professional life.

For anyone who desires a positive attitude, there is going to be a need to be committed enough to cultivate it.

He says that "the most valuable asset you can possess is a positive attitude toward your life." He argues that if a person changes his thinking, he can change his beliefs. He further believes that by changing one's beliefs, then that person can change his actions. And finally by changing one's actions, then that person can change his life.

Your attitude has the ability to influence your entire personal and professional life. What we think about the most has the ability to influence the way we feel, thereby influencing our attitude.

> *Your attitude has the ability to influence your entire personal and professional life.*

Our life are constantly heading in the direction of our dominant thought life, that is to say, healthy and positive thoughts propel us into developing a positive attitude and the reverse is true where unhealthy and negative thoughts are concerned.

A person's attitude can either be a powerful means for positive action –or can stifle one's ability to fulfill his or her potential.

Although we cannot control the circumstances that befall us, we can decide to choose how we respond to those circumstances. While people with a positive attitude are influenced by what goes on within them, those with a negative attitude are influenced by what goes on around them. He mentions that one of the ways our circumstances can be improved upon is by improving our response to them.

According to Norman Vincent Peale in his book **The power of the plus factor**[18]. "The positive thinker is an optimistic, faith-motivated person who habitually projects positive images and attitude every day, sending creative and positive thoughts into the world around him. These strong thought waves condition the surrounding world positively and positive outcomes are activated"

CULTIVATING A POSITIVE ATTITUDE TO LIFE

While cultivating a positive attitude, I have come to realise that giving up is not an option if you want to achieve anything significant in life. Whether it is a goal of being a more committed Christian, a successful student, or a successful entrepreneur, you have to choose to be committed to pursuing your cause never to give up, no matter what.

You should behave like a leech. When a leech attaches itself to a creature with a view to sucking its blood, it is difficult to let go the creature until it succeeds.

My policy has always been that when I start something, I want to go with it all the way to the end despite the bumps and humps along the way. You should never stop until you reach your destination. You also need to cultivate patience in the process of pursuing your goal.

---

[18] Peale, Vincent Norman (1987) *The power of the plus factor*. New Jersey, Fleming. H Renel Company,

ADJUSTING YOUR MENTAL ATTITUDE

One way through which negative attitude manifests in our live is how we deal with offence. Handling offences is very important in the adjustment of our attitude.

One of the things that help me in adjusting my attitude especially when dealing with offence is applying the Golden Rule- Do unto Others as You Would Want Them to Do You.

Being easily offended opens a door to negative attitudes. Regardless of who we are, all of us have opportunities to be offended by our loved ones, co-workers or people around us at any given moment in time.

No one is exempted from dealing with offence. Therefore, how you and I choose to react to offence is what makes the difference. Since we all want to be forgiven and loved when we fall short of other people's expectations, forgiveness is what we need to offer those who fail us or annoy us in various ways.

You may say, "But Sammy, you do not know what that person did to me." Well the truth is that I may not know the gravity of the hurt and pain and I am not in any way trying to make light of it. However, the truth of the matter is entertaining bitterness, resentment and unforgiveness opens a door to negativity and it is devastating in the long run. There is nothing exciting about its consequences! Therefore, let forgiveness be your watch word.

> The most valuable asset you can possess is a positive attitude toward your life.

SEEING THE BIG PICTURE

I have learnt through the years that once you decide to achieve a given goal, you do not really need to figure out all the details as to how it is going to happen. Setting targets and taking one step at a time has enabled me to stay calm, on course and focused even in the midst of discouragement.

Always putting what I refer to as the "big picture" before me, coupled with dedication and commitment to achieving my goal has actually helped me to stay focused.

Another thing that has helped me to stay optimistic is the fact that despite the challenges, no situation is permanent. In other words, whatever has a beginning must have an end as well.

If you have no picture of the future, there is no way you can have a positive attitude towards life. You need a very bright vision of where you intend to be, for you to overlook the depressing situation at present.

It takes a great vision to live through a period of joblessness and still keep your spirit high. Vision elicits joy and produces a positive attitude towards life.

Most people do fail in life because they do not think the thoughts and do the things that will change their circumstances. As for me, I refuse to be a failure in life so I constantly make deliberate adjustments in my thought patterns and embark on thinking about what is positive instead.

I close this chapter with this short story:

TWO SEEDS

Two seeds lay side by side in the fertile soil.

The first seed said, "I want to grow! I want to send my roots deep into the soil beneath me and thrust my sprouts through the earth's crust above me ... I want to unfurl my tender buds like banners to announce the arrival of a new life... I want to feel the warmth of the sun on my face and the blessing of the morning dew on my petals!"

And so she grew...

The second seed said, "Hmmmm. If I send my roots into the ground below, I don't know what I will encounter in the dark. If I push my way through the hard soil above me I may damage my delicate sprouts ... what if I let my buds open and a snail tries to eat them? And if I were to open my blossoms, a small child may pull me from the ground. No, it is much better for me to wait until it is safe."

And so she waited...

A yard hen scratching around the ground for food found the waiting seed and promptly ate it.

"Your attitude determines your altitude"

LIFE PRINCIPLE FROM CHAPTER FOUR

- *Attitude is an inward feeling expressed by behaviour.*
- *For anyone who desires a positive attitude, there is going to be a need to be committed enough to cultivate it.*
- *An attitude of defeat or panic applies pressure on the blood vessels and has a debilitating effect on the entire endocrine system.*
- *You also need to cultivate patience in the process of pursuing your goal.*
- *If you have no picture of the future, there is no way you can have a positive attitude toward life. Your attitude has the ability to influence your entire personal and professional life.*

CHAPTER 5

"The brain is like a muscle. When it is use we feel very good."
-Carl Sagan

CHAPTER FIVE

THE PRODUCTS OF A LOADED BRAIN

"Empty pockets never held anyone back. Only empty heads and empty hearts can do that."
-Norman Vincent Pearl

The brain is the most complex organ in the human body; it is the organ of creativity and the seat of intelligence. Everything that we see today emerged from the brain. But the brain is only as good as its content. The things stored in the brain determine the value of a person. It is not the size of the head that counts, but the quality of information stored in the brain and how it is utilized.

For instance, a tall handsome young man who is insane will never be counted during census, because his brain is not in good order, he is not considered as a citizen. He cannot contribute to the development of the nation; he is not an asset but rather a liability.

It is the use of the brain that determines the worth of a man, not the beauty of his face or the size of his chest muscles.

YOUR THREE BRAINS

According to a research done by Jeff Gee and Val Gee in their book, *The Winner's Attitude: Change How You Deal* with *Difficult People and Get the BEST Out of Any Situation*[19], they posited that we all have three type of brains;

i. The reptilian brain,

ii. The animal brain (also known as the limbic system or mammalian brain), and

iii. The human brain (also known as the neocortex or cerebral cortex).

Between the animal and the human brain lies the reticular activating system which is a kind of toggle switch that resides deep inside the brain and connects to all the feelings it gets throughout the mind and body. It is believed that the switch has the ability to turn on the operating system depending on what stimulus it receives.

> It is not the size of the head that counts, but the quality of information stored in the brain.

THE REPTILIAN BRAIN AND THE ANIMAL BRAIN

The reptilian brain is the one that enables our bodies to do so much multitasking processes such as the process of seeing, hearing, heartbeat, metabolism, among others, without our being aware of it.

The animal brain surrounds your reptilian brain and it also focuses on your well-being. All animals have an animal brain and we, the human animal are no exception.

---

[19] Gee, Jeff & Gee, Val (2006), *The Winner's Attitude: Change How You Deal with Difficult People and Get the BEST Out of Any Situation.* New York: McGraw-Hill companies.

The animal brain is about one thing and one thing only: survival! It is born in fear, lives in fear, and dies in fear. Its main job is to endeavor to keep us alive and out of danger. The animal brain is always on the lookout to ensure that it is not being taken advantage of, and it has the ability to keep a record of things people say, just to "get them" later.

Jeff Gee and Val Gee have made the following deductions pertaining to the animal brain:

- It has a tendency to justify everything.
- It lacks any sense of humor.
- It prefers to go into hiding for fear of danger.
- It lives in an environment of fear and will do anything to create it.
- It reminds you of things you did in the past so that you feel guilty and bad.
- It reminds you of things other people did to you in the past that hurt you.
- It will nag you about things in the future so that you feel worried and uncertain about tomorrow.

Jeff Gee and Val Gee suggest that you can ensure that you do not operate from the animal brain by engaging the following two steps:

    i. Realise you are operating from the animal brain.

    ii. Switch to your human brain.

ANIMAL BRAIN IGNITERS

Jeff Gee and Val Gee suppose that if you are having any thoughts, feelings, or actions associated with the following words below, you are probably operating from the animal brain unawares:

Prideful, Frustrated, Judgmental, Greedy, Bored, Angry, Envious, Depressed, Worrying, Superior Suspicious, Embarrassed, Lying, Arrogant, Jealous, Guilty, Cruel, Destructive, Selfish, Resentful Possessive, Critical, Uncertain

THE HUMAN BRAIN

According to Jeff Gee and Val Gee we have a human brain that surrounds the animal brain. This is what causes us to operate from love, acceptance, peace, and understanding. It is this brain that allows us to share, help a co-worker, volunteer, and respect and honor other people. They maintain that the human brain is different from the animal brain because it operates not from the dark and low level of fear and survival kind of life, but from a higher level. It is born in love, lives in love, and dies in love.

LOVE AND THE HUMAN BRAIN

Jeff Gee and Val Gee are of the view that whereas in the animal brain there are sides and positions to hold, in the human brain there is connectedness and the Golden Rule: *"Treat others as you would have them treat you."* The innermost longing of every human being is to love and be loved.

They assert that the Golden Rule does not say *"you have to believe in the same thing that I believe in"* or *"you have to have the same colour of skin that I do"* or *"you have to come from the same land or have the same kind of education or history."*

In the light of the Golden Rule principle, Jeff and Val maintain that whether you are a customer, co-worker, spouse, son, daughter, parent, friend, or stranger, you want one main thing and that is love.

PULLING THE TRIGGER OF THE HUMAN BRAIN

Jeff Gee and Val Gee are of the view that the following list of emotions, feelings, and actions can only be activated in the human brain. If any of the following words describe you then you are probably operating from the human brain as per their research.

Giving, Accepting, Truthful, Tolerant, Take action, Concerned, Reliable, Open, Optimistic, Purposeful, Considerate, Gentle, Trusting, Inspired, Thoughtful, Honest, Peaceful, Humorous, Helpful, Joyful, Patient, Generous, Modest, Encouraging, Warm, Loving, Appreciation.

TABULAR RASA

At birth the human brain is presumed to be empty, a phenomenon in philosophy and psychology known as *tabular rasa* which means that whatever is written on that plain empty mind is what the person ultimately grow up to become. As we advance through life, from infancy to adulthood, the brain begins to acquire all sort of information that determines the survival of the individual.

The information that gets to the brain has two main sources:
    i. Education and
    ii. Experience

In the first chapter, I said that perception is what determines reality. Perception is not genetically conferred, it is acquired.

You were not born with any point of view; your point of view is a product of your interaction with your environment.

The building blocks of our perception are the education we acquire and the experiences that we have as we go through life.

> The building blocks of our perception are the education we acquire and the experiences that we have as we go through life.

Education and experience allow an individual to build respect from other people for whatever he does.

One of the ultimate of life is to learn. Learning is an avenue for the brain to be loaded with the right information. No one can live life without learning something.

What you learn and experience can often determine your success or failure in life. Learning combined with real life experience is a winning formula for success. Your choices and your experiences help create the person that you are.

Arthur Conan Doyle in his book "**A Study in Scarlet**[20]" made the following assertion about the brain:

> *"I consider that a man's brain originally is like a little empty attic, and you have to stock it with such furniture as you choose. A fool takes in all the lumber of every sort that he comes across, so that the knowledge which might be*

---

[20] Doyle, Arthur Conan. (1887) " *A Study In Scarlet*" Ward, Lock and Co. UK

> *useful to him gets crowded out, or at best is jumbled up with a lot of other things, so that he has a difficulty in laying his hands upon it. Now the skillful workman is very careful indeed as to what he takes into his brain-attic. He will have nothing but the tools which may help him in doing his work, but of these he has a large assortment, and all in the most perfect order. It is a mistake to think that, that little room has elastic walls and can distend to any extent. Depend upon it there comes a time when for every addition of knowledge you forget something that you knew before. It is of the highest importance, therefore, not to have useless facts elbowing out the useful ones."*

One of the reasons why I love Schooling is that it provides a platform for learning and the acquisition of education, but school attendance does not necessarily confer education on an individual.

It is possible for an individual to attend school without getting an education. Examples abound of graduates who attended school, but lack the requisite life surviving skill that education confers.

THE POCKET AND THE BRAIN

When we talk about the pocket and the brain, people have different notions; some believe that brainy people are seldom wealthy, while others believe in the reverse.

A brainy person might not be in Forbes list of world's richest people, notwithstanding that person will however live a very comfortable life and always have money in his pocket to meet the basic needs of life.

It is therefore not possible for an individual's brain to be loaded with relevant up-to-date information and his pocket or bank account is empty. If one claim to be

Wake up! Take This Job!

brainy and his pocket or bank account is always empty, the content of his brain has to be examined to ascertain what he really has in his brain.

The content of one's pocket speaks volume about an individual's knowledge base. An empty pocket could be a sign of an empty brain. Every man that has his pocket or bank account full of cash today has a story of several hours of brain work - of utilizing the information loaded in his brain.

As an individual, I particularly believe that life seldom gives you what you deserve; life only gives you what you place a demand on life to give to you. Such demand starts by tasking the brain. When you place a demand on your brain, it will definitely produce for you.

I conclude this chapter with this short story about a lion, a jackal and a donkey.

The Donkey's Brain.
Long ago in the forest lived a lion. He had a jackal as his partner. They both always went together for hunting. The lion used to kill the animals and the jackal got his share for helping the lion then and there.

One day, the lion fell sick. He could not go out. But he was very hungry. He called the jackal and said, "Dear friend, I am hungry. But, I am too sick to hunt. You have to help me get some food".

The jackal went off in search of prey. He found a donkey at last. He said to the donkey, "Hello, Donkey Sir! The king of the forest wants to make you his minister". The foolish donkey was too happy to think of the plot. He followed the jackal. The lion killed the donkey. But, before eating, he felt so thirsty. He said to the jackal, "Take care of the donkey. I will return in no time".

As soon as the lion left, the jackal started eating the brain of the donkey. When the lion returned he found the donkey's brain missing.

He asked the jackal. "Where is the donkey's brain?"
The jackal answered timidly, "If he had a brain would he have come here?"[21]

If I Only Had a Brain
"I could while away the hours
Conferring with the flowers
Consulting with the rain.
And my head I'd be a-scratchin'
While my thoughts were busy hatchin'
If I only had a brain."

- **Sung by the Scarecrow in *The Wizard of Oz***

George A. Dorsey has this to say about the use of the brain: *"The more you use your brain, the more brain you will have to use."* Putting your brain to work is necessary for you to gain relevance on earth. When you put your brain to work you will begin to generate revenue. You cannot be generating revenue and have an empty pocket or bank account.

---

[21] Retrieved from www.english-for-students.com/brain/html

LIFE PRINCIPLES FROM CHAPTER FIVE

- *It is not the size of the head that counts, but the quality of information stored in the brain.*
- *The building blocks of our perception are the education we acquire and the experiences that we have as we go through life*
- *An empty pocket could be seen as a sign of an empty brain.*
- *One of the ultimate meanings of life is to learn*
- *The more you use your brain, the more brain you will have to use.*

Wake up! Take This Job!

CHAPTER

6

"Every day is a bank account, and time is our currency. No one is rich, no one is poor, and we have got 24 hours each"
-Christopher Rice

CHAPTER SIX

PERSONAL REVENUE GENERATION

"Money is the last enemy that shall never be subdued. While there is flesh there is money or the want of money, but money is always on the brain so long as there is a brain in reasonable order."
-Samuel Butler

The President of the Federal Republic of Nigeria, made a striking remark during the 28th convocation ceremony of the University of Port Harcourt. The President, who was represented by the Minister of Education, Prof. Ruqayyatu Ahmed Rufa'i, stated that the graduands had been fully equipped to be able to stand as self-reliant individuals. He said: **"Be generators of employment, rather than populating the unemployment market. Seek opportunities for entrepreneurial engagements."**

This is coming straight from the President's mouth. He was stressing the need for young people to engage in entrepreneurial pursuit.

After graduation, the next most logical thing you must strive to do is something that will generate revenue for you. You need to be engaged in something that will put money in your pocket. You need to earn or etch a living.

Wake up! Take This Job!

You need to make ends meet. Revenue generation is not optional for you, you really do not have a choice, and it is either you seek ways to generate revenue or you are doomed to beg or borrow to survive.

> After graduation, the next most logical thing you must strive to do is something that will generate revenue for you. Something that will put money in your pocket.

If you choose to beg, you will soon find out that beggars are not always welcome and borrowers are not always liked by people.

By the time you are through with begging all your friends, family members and relatives, will be tired of your incessant requests for money for recharge cards, transportation, for barbing or hairdo and other things. One day they will tell you either to your face or by their attitude that they cannot tolerate your begging any more.

They will tell you to go and get something to do. Then it will dawn on you that you really need to generate revenue. The import of this book is to aid you to spot and take advantage of means of revenue that are often neglected by most graduates.

WHAT IS REVENUE GENERATION?

Revenue generation is the process by which an individual secures financial resources for his/her survival, sustenance and security. There are two major types of income.

UNEARNED AND EARNED INCOME

1. **Unearned**: This is income that comes to you that you do not necessarily labour for such as monetary or non-monetary gifts.

Wake up! Take This Job!

2. **Earned income**: is income earned when an individual provides service or product for which a fee is charged. This category is the main thrust of this book.

When I discuss about income in particular with my friends who are searching for jobs, I always prefer the term Revenue Generation, I use the term "**Revenue Generation**" because it is both an art and an act. It is an art because it is an ability that can be acquired by training; it is an act, because it requires action. It requires you to put whatever you have learnt to work.

Therefore, the art and act of generating revenue should penetrate every fibre of your being and saturate every aspect of your life both now and even when you start making big money.

> *Revenue does not just come to you; it will not drop on you like a mango from a mango tree. You have to go out there and get it.*

Revenue does not just come to you; it will not drop on you like a mango from a mango tree. You have to go out there and get it. Like the proverbial saying "money does not grow on trees" that is very true, even if it does, you have to climb the tree to pluck it.

PLANTING YOUR OWN MONEY TREE

It is said, according to a Chinese Myth:

"The owner of a money tree will have good luck and fortune brought upon him".

The problem is how are you going to get a tree whose leaves are naira notes? With the increase rate of deforestation, even if there was to be a money tree somewhere, by now it would have been extinct; therefore, laying your hands on one might be a very difficult, if not an impossible task.

But if you desperately want to be a proud owner of a money tree, you must take the responsibility of planting your own.

You can plant your own money tree by starting a revenue generating venture. With a venture that constantly generate revenue, you are sure of having money, and if you persist enough in it you might have a surplus of wealth. Yet, nurturing this money tree (venture) to prosper and grow will be impossible without creating a strong root system. You will have to work hard.

Money will not fall like manna from heaven, it must be generated. It must be generated by working on something that is worthwhile and profitable. You must be engaged doing something tangible for you to generate substantial revenue.

To generate revenue requires some form of input; of ideas, energy, time, money and a great deal of patience. It is the quality of input that determines the quality of your output (financial return).

For you not to become a liability to your family and society, you must know how to generate revenue with what you have and from where you are. Revenue generation has nothing to do with your degree, age or grade.

In fact, people will begin to wonder at you if with your level of education you cannot generate substantial revenue to take care of yourself and take up some responsibilities around you.

There are ten crucial reasons why you need to generate revenue for yourself. These are vital; you cannot push them aside. It is either you do or you are subjected to to the dishonourable world of begging and borrowing.

TEN FUNDAMENTAL REASONS WHY YOU MUST GENERATE REVENUE (INCOME)

"Who escapes a duty avoids a gain"
- Theodore Eliot

i. **For personal upkeep:**

The first reason why you need to work is for personal upkeep.

Personal means belonging to a particular person rather than a group or an Organisation. For example, personal bank account, personal computer, personal identification number, etc. The efficient management of personal effects lies solely on the owner. Therefore we must take reasonable care to manage and safeguard our personal assets or personhood.

Upkeep is described by the Advance Learner English Dictionary as "The cost and process of keeping something in good condition."

I love this definition, because without cost there can not be upkeep. Wherever there is cost, money comes into play. Upkeep therefore means the money you need to take care of yourself. It further said that upkeep is a process. It is not what you do today and it is over, it is something that you must continue to do.

Wake up! Take This Job!

As soon as you graduate out of school, there are some personal responsibilities you must shoulder, even if you are still living with your parent, you must be responsible for your personal upkeep.

You need to take care of yourself; nobody will do it for you. For some personal things like barbing your hair or making your hair(for the ladies), buying recharge cards, transportation, buying your body cream, perfumes, body spray and clothes. You need revenue to take care of these things.

If you still go to your parents for money to buy these basic things, then you have a serious problem. It is a slight on your graduate status for you to depend on your parents, girl friend or boy friend, or any other person for your personal upkeep.

The matter of personal upkeep gets even more serious if you are living on your own. You have to pay house rent, light bill, water bill (remember you buy sachet water), feed yourself, make your house presentable. All these will not fall from heaven, money must speak. Revenue must be generated to take care of them.

> *The evidence that you love yourself is that you take good care of yourself. And taking good care of yourself requires money.*

The scripture says **"love your neighbor as you love yourself."** The evidence that you love yourself is that you take good care of yourself and taking good care of yourself requires money.

ii. To Preserve Your Dignity

Nothing robs an individual of his dignity like begging and borrowing. Begging and borrowing reduce a man, diminish his worth and undermines his ability. Only work can restores such a person's worth. Naturally, a graduate commands respect in the society, but after a while if you stay too long without a source of income, your respect begins to diminish. And if nothing is done to redeem it, you will lose all the respect that you have.

Earning a living is better than begging for a living. No matter how little the money you earn, you command respect from both friends and foes. That is why it is commonly said that there is dignity in labour. On the other hand it could be equally said that there is indignity in idleness.

If you are generating revenue for yourself, you will command the respect of people. People naturally respect a hard working man. If you are working, no matter the kind of work, it is better than begging.

Your worth is not measured by your certificate but by your works. If you have a good certificate and you are not working, you are not any better than a person without a certificate. In fact, a person without a certificate that is working is better than a man with a certificate and has nothing to show for his certificate.

> Earning a living is better than begging for a living.

Borrowing also lowers one's dignity. The scripture tells us that a borrower is a servant to the lender. Borrowing is a dangerous trap, it is even more dangerous for a man without a job, and you end up owing people without a hope of repaying. Debt is a financial blockage which could have a great effect on your financial future, because you have to pay your debt before you think of saving.

iii. **For Future Investment**
"So with severe famine everywhere in the land, Joseph opened up the store houses and sold grain to the Egyptians. And the people from surrounding lands also came to Egypt to buy grain from Joseph because the famine was severe throughout the world."
-Genesis 41: 56-57

Revenue generation creates a pool for future investment. From my interaction with graduates, I discovered that most of them have great ideas and lofty dreams but these dreams might just end up as dreams without funds.

Owing to some factors, it might be very difficult to get funds to fledge a novel idea. Funds are provided by financial institutions for ideas that have materialised and probably need expansion.

This situation places you and your idea in a tight corner. It becomes necessary for you as the visionary, to get to work to save some money that you can commit to your idea and invest into your future.

Revenue generation enables you to put away something for the future. If you are not generating revenue, your bank account will always be empty, with an empty bank account, how can you possibly invest in the future?

iv. **To Support Your Family Members**
While you were in school, your family supported you. Now that you are a graduate, you are expected to support your family. You have to reciprocate the kind gesture shown to you by your family. You cannot support your family without money.

If you stay too long without generating revenue, your family might begin to feel that their investment into your life is a waste. Whether your parents demand for support or not, you have to use your discretion once in a while to show some appreciation. You need to prove to them that you are indeed a responsible child. For this reason alone, you have to step out of the house and get to work.

v.   To Advance The Kingdom Of God On Earth
If you are a true Christian, you should know that kingdom advancement is a priority. The kingdom of God will not be sponsored by those who do not belong to the kingdom. It is the citizen of God kingdom that will finance the kingdom projects, if you are a true citizen of God's kingdom, then you must be involve in a revenue generating venture, so that you can support the work of God. No matter how small your contribution is it is necessary that you have money to give for God's work to advance.

There are missions to be sponsored; pastor's to be cared for; churches to be built and lost souls to be won into the kingdom. All these require a whole lot of cash. The earlier you start generating revenue the better for the kingdom of God.

vi.   To Get A Better Education
Education is a continuum. For you to advance in life, you must continue to upgrade your educational status. You will need to get higher degree and you will be solely responsible for it, except of course if you win a scholarship or if your parents have enough to take care of your post graduate studies. Good education is very, very expensive; therefore, you need to generate revenue for you to get a good higher education.

vii. To Enhance The Quality Of Your Life

There is a better life, much better than the one you are presently experiencing.

Scripture says
> *"But the path of the [uncompromisingly] just {and} righteous is like the light of dawn, that shines more and more (brighter and clearer) until [it reaches its full strength and glory in] the perfect day [to be prepared]."*
> - Proverbs 4:18(AMP)

"Things will get better" is a popular axiom among youths in Nigeria, but you have to start working for things to be better. Otherwise you could wait for the rest of your life and not get any better than you are now. To enhance the quality of your life, you must start working. And you should start now! You must begin to generate revenue for yourself.

The good things of this life do not come on a platter of gold, they require work. Without a revenue generating venture, you may not get the better life that you dream of. Graduates daydream a lot, they dream of the big cars, the luxury house, and the beautiful things that they wish to have. But you know that, if wishes were horses beggars would ride. The good life will not materialise by mere wishing and faithless confession. It requires more than that. It requires real work.

> *If you are not generating revenue, your bank account and pocket will always be empty.*

Among some of the things that will enhance the quality of your life is marriage. And it is necessary that you generate revenue to take care of it.

viii. To Add Value To Society

Society will remain undeveloped if revenue is not generated by the citizens. All the infrastructure and symbols of civilization that we see around us today are evidence of revenue generation. Society thrives on mutual contribution from the citizenry in form of taxation. To add value to society you must generate revenue. You need a venture that will bring money to you, so that you can contribute your quota to the development of your community and the nation at large.

> *"As you add value to yourself, you are adding value to society"*
> -E.E. Ukeredi

ix. It Is A Divine Command

When it comes to the issue of revenue generation, you really do not have a choice because it is a command from the Lord. A command is not something that you can push aside or negotiate. It is either you do it or you are doomed.

The scripture says,

> **"For even when we were with you, we gave you this rule:** *"If a man will not work, he shall not eat."*
> - 2 Thessalonians 3:10

The Master is saying "Go and generate revenue for yourself."

x. To Give To The Poor

The scripture says that "the poor will always be in our midst". It is either you are in the begging business or you are in the giving business. The problem is that there are more beggars than givers. But whether you are a beggar or a giver is absolutely dependent on you. The giving side is the winning side, for you to be on the giving side, you must generate revenue by being gainfully engaged. Work is the underlying factor that determines whether you end up as a beggar or a giver.

> The giving side is the winning side.

There are poor people everywhere and poor people more often than not are on the begging side, so you must step out of the poverty circle and work so that you can give generously to them.

I conclude this chapter with this conversation between a fisherman and a businessman

THE FISHERMAN AND THE BUSINESSMAN

Once upon a time, there lived a fisherman and his family along the coast.

One day the fisherman was lying on the beautiful beach with his fishing pole propped up in the sand.

He was enjoying the warmth of the afternoon sun and the prospect of catching a fish.

About that time, a businessman came walking down the beach trying to relieve some of the stress of his workday. He noticed the fisherman sitting on the beach and decided to find out why this fisherman was sitting instead of working harder to make a living for himself and his family.

"You are not going to catch many fish that way," said the businessman to the fisherman, "you should be working rather than lying on the beach!"

The fisherman looked up at the businessman, smiled and replied, "And what will my reward be?"

"Well, you can get bigger nets and catch more fish!" was the businessman's answer.

"And then what will my reward be?" asked the fisherman, still smiling.

The businessman replied, "You will make money and you will be able to buy a boat which will then result in larger catches of fish!"

"And then what will my reward be?" asked the fisherman again.

The businessman was beginning to get a little irritated with the fisherman's questions.

"You can buy a bigger boat and hire some people to work for you!" he said.

"And then what will my reward be?" repeated the fisherman.

The businessman was getting angry. "Don't you understand? You can build up a fleet of fishing boats, sail all over the world, and let all your employees catch fish for you!"

Once again the fisherman asked, "And then what will my reward be?"

The businessman was red with rage and shouted at the fisherman,

"Don't you understand that you can become so rich that you will never have to work for your living again? You can spend all the rest of your days sitting on this beach looking at the sunset. You will not have a care in the world!"

Wake up! Take This Job!

Are you like the fisherman that is armed with his fishing gears and lying on the beach instead of using it to catch fish?

I think this quote from the United States President, Barack Obama is very appropriate to close this chapter.

"Money is not the only answer, but it makes a

LIFE PRINCIPLES FROM CHAPTER SIX

- *After graduation, the next most logical thing you must strive to do is something that will generate revenue for you. Something that will put money in your pocket.*
- *Revenue does not just come to you; it will not drop on you like a mango from a mango tree. You have to go out there and get it.*
- *The evidence that you love yourself is that you take good care of yourself. And taking good care of yourself requires money.*
- *Nothing robs an individual of his dignity like begging and borrowing. Begging and borrowing reduces a man, diminishes his worth and undermines his ability.*
- *Earning a living is better than begging for a living.*
- *It is either you are in the begging business or you are in the giving business.*
- *If you are not generating revenue, your bank account will always be empty.*
- *The giving side is the winning side.*

CHAPTER

7

"Education is not preparation for life; education is life itself."
-John Dewey

CHAPTER SEVEN

LEARNING FOR LIVING

"Formal education will make you a living; self education will make you a fortune"
-Jim Rohn

Now that you know why you need to generate revenue, it is also important that you know how to generate it. The scripture says

"The labour of the foolish wearieth every one of them, because they do not know how to get to the city"
-Ecclesiastics 10:15(KJV)

Most graduates are like the foolish in the above scripture. They know that the city has great prospect for prosperity, but has no idea about how to get to the city. They are often confused, not knowing what to do and where to go. The **"how"** is what I call "strategy". Strategy is a plan that is based on up-to-date and relevant information.

The takeoff point for revenue generation is not the development of a plan. Most times we attempt to develop plans without the requisite information that form the blueprint. That is more like jumping the gun.

The first step in the development of a strategy for revenue generation is the acquisition of information, by information I mean awareness and education.

The unalloyed truth that you should know is that revenue generation is not solely based on your certificate as some people would want you to believe, but it rest unshakably on the education you have acquired. Knowledge therefore is the key to revenue generation, and not certificate.

EDUCATION CAN DO WHAT CERTIFICATE CANNOT DO

The Universal Declaration of Human Rights adopted by the United Nations General Assembly in December 1948[22] guaranteed for the individual a whole range of basic freedom with education serving as a basic right necessary for the achievement of all other freedoms.

The achievement of the right to education requires that young people be given the opportunity necessary for the acquisition of the knowledge, skills, attitudes and values which will enable them lead happy and productive lives as individuals and discharge their social duties for the betterment of life in the society. But whether we are getting such education in Nigeria is a question that has to be answered.

PAPER QUALIFICATION VERSUS PERSONALITY DEVELOPMENT

"Of all knowledge the wise and the good seek most to know themselves"
-William Shakespeare

Please I want you to be frank with this question: Which would you prefer of the following, being given a certificate for a course you never attended or being given life surviving skills without any certificate to show that you have had the training?

---

[22] Available at: www.**un**.org/en/documents/udhr/index.shtml

Many would prefer to amass certificates that they never had training for. Hoping that their certificate will take them to where they wish to be.

Again, which is more valuable? Is it the paper or the person that owns the paper? Some people will say the paper, but I strongly believe that the person is better than the paper because in the absence of the paper the person can thrive, but the paper will rot without the person.

THE ON GOING WAR

When you hear of war what to your mind? When there is a threat of war how do you feel? Are you overwhelmed with great trepidation or do you just act as if nothing is going on?

What if I tell you that we are at war in Nigeria and nobody is worried about it? Indeed we are at war. This war is not like any that you have seen, heard or read about. It is more catastrophic than the Nigerian civil war. And if we are not careful our very existence, identity and future might be consumed by it.

Paper qualification is at war with personality development in Nigeria? This war has been ongoing, quietly and steady. But in recent times it has assume monstrous proportion and has taken centre stage.

The war is fierce and the casualties cut across every stratum. Every aspect of our nation and the very fabric of our society have been shred to piece by the war.

This war has crippled our reasoning capacity, mutilated our creative ingenuity, undermines our intellectual competence and weakens our competitive advantage among the comity of nations.

Wake up! Take This Job!

This war rages from the public sector to the private sector; from the office to the factory; from the bedroom to the boardroom; from the pulpit to the pew; from the government to the governed; from the elected to the electorate and from the teachers to students.

There are casualties everywhere. Personality development is being slaughtered for paper qualification and character is being crucified for credentials.

Going by what we read in the newspapers and what we hear in the news, it seems that paper qualification is winning the war.

When I was growing up I was told that education is the development of the individual both in character and in learning. This belief was reenacted in my days in the University but, that is not what is obtainable today. We have placed a higher premium on paper qualification and undermine the importance of development of our personality.

From what I see around me, it is like character development is no longer part of our educational curriculum. It is more like gaining the whole world and losing your soul. We desire good certificate, without a strong character. What do we get in the long run? Graduates who cannot defend what they claim to have acquired.

"The end and aim of all education is the development of character."
- Francis W. Parker

GETTING A CERTIFICATE IS EASY, CHARACTER DEVELOPMENT IS HARD

Wake up! Take This Job!

Just about anyone in Nigeria can get a certificate, but only the truly conscientious gets an education. From nursery school to the University, we crave for certificate at the expense of education. Nobody cares about how you get your A's in your WAEC and NECO or how you scored 280 and above in JAMB, it is even inconsequential how you get your second class upper, all that count is that you have a certificate.

This situation accounts for the man-power challenge we are having in this country, because a large chunk of our graduates have good certificates, with little or no education. It has been said that Nigerian graduates are half baked. What it means is that our graduates are armed with good certificates without the corresponding education and without a strong character.

To drive home the point I am making, let me refer to an interview in the Vanguard newspaper of Thursday May 17, 2012. In that interview the Executive Director of 7UP Bottling Company Plc, Mr. Femi Mokikan, talked about an aptitude test that was conducted in his company (7UP) for prospective job seekers. He said that the first question in the quantitative section was to compute mean, mode, median of some given data.

> Paper qualification is at war with personality development.

He said there was a man who said he had Bsc Mathematics/Statistics, and won an award, but failed the question and even failed the test. Mr. Femi Mokikan said he insisted that they invite him for the interview, because he could not understand why a Bsc graduate of Mathematics/Statistics could not solve for mean, mode and median.

So, the man came for the interview, Mr. Mokikan said he asked him if he could recall any of the questions especially in the quantitative section. He said he could. Then he was asked how he calculated it, upon further questioning the man figured out that something was not right and he said he was no longer interested in the job. Mr. Mokikan told him that he must continue and asked him of the true owner of the result. All the man could say was "Oga, just let me go."

It is obvious that the gentle man did not personally work to earn his degree; or how else can we explain the above scenario. He probably bought it with money. The truth is that many just pay for results.

Ironically, we expect our dear country Nigeria to be transformed by graduates of such configuration. It cannot happen. It is like going to the well to fetch water with a basket.

It is not possible for people with certificate but without education to transform society; it is those with good and applicable education that can bring the change that we crave for.

"Only the educated are free"
- Epictetus

WHAT IS WRONG WITH WHAT WE CALL EDUCATION?

Education is widely regarded as being central, if not the primary driver, of socio-economic development all over the world, because it holds the potential of connecting people with opportunities that can improve their livelihoods. With all that education promises, how come we are not making the most of our educational experience in Nigeria? Something must be wrong with our version of education?

So, what is wrong with our education? The Nigeria system of education emphasizes theories instead of values, concepts rather than human beings, abstraction rather than consciousness, answers instead of questions, ideology and efficiency rather than conscience. It stresses on certificate instead of knowledge and technical know-how; it emphasizes paper qualification instead of personality development; it celebrates the accumulation of credentials instead of character formation and it places premium on good grades instead of the ability to trade.

Egba in his book *"The Impact of Business Studies in Schools. A Hand Book on Practical Business in Schools[23]"* asserted that **Nigeria has promoted the idea that the only good education is an education capped with many years in a University. This ideas, transmitted by our values, our aspirations, is snobbish, undemocratic, and a revelation of why our schools disappoint so many students, both in character and in learning.**

In consideration of what Education is supposed to do Nneji in his work on *"The impact of Business school in Nigeria[24]* said that education *"**Is supposed to prepare an individual for a career in life. Unfortunately, most Nigerian children go into various stages of education, right from the primary to tertiary institutions without any preparation for whatever career stages they aim at"**.

---

[23] Egba, S. P. (2010): *The Impact of Business Studies in Schools.* A Hand Book on Practical Business in Schools. Akpos Learning Publishers, Port Harcourt.

[24] Nneji S.P (1999): The Impact of Business in Nigeria, *Pearl Journal of Business & Management*, Vol.6, No. 2 P. 6-12.

Wake up! Take This Job!

Today, there are many graduates without jobs while there are many jobs without people to do them.

Why is it like this? The reason is that we often see certificate as an end; and schooling as a means to that end.

This is very wrong; the school is a platform for you to get an education. The goal of education is not mastery of subject matter, but of one's person. Subject matter is simply the tool. Much as a good sculpture one would use a hammer and chisel to carve a block of marble, one uses ideas and knowledge to forge one's own personality.

For the most part we struggle under a confusion of ends and means, thinking that the purpose of education is to ensure that we get a certificate and we see that certificate as our meal ticket. This perception is wrong. As long as we hold on to this perception we are likely to miss the gains of schooling.

EDUCATION IS LIFE
"Education is not preparation for life; education is life itself".
-John Dewey

Education is the totality of life experience that you acquire and which enables you to cope with and derive satisfaction from living in this world. This is because it enables you to achieve social competence and optimum fulfillment.

Education acquaints you with the lessons of the human race and conveys the messages of life to you as a student in the school of life. Education is very necessary for every human being, without it a man may not be able to make the best of his life's journey.

> *"Education will shape the world of tomorrow — it is the most effective means that society possesses for confronting the challenges of the future. Progress increasingly depends upon educated minds: upon research, invention, innovation and adaptation. Educated minds and instincts are needed not only in laboratories and research institutes, but also in every walk of life. While education is not the whole answer to every problem, in its broadest sense, education must be a vital part of all efforts to imagine and create new relations among people and to foster greater respect for the needs of the environment"[25].*

Education does not mean to get specific skill and get employment. But we say that somebody got education, if he has developed from every angle. It means you have developed in every ramification.

I was told that in those days an educated person is seen as someone who knows something about everything. That is to say that such a person has developed in every respect. But the reverse is the case today.

> *"The essence of all education is self-discovery and self-control. When education helps an individual to discover his own powers and limitations and, shows him how to get out of his heredity its largest and best possibilities, it will fulfill its real function, when children are taught not merely to know things but particularly to know themselves, not merely how to do things but especially how to compel themselves to do things, they may be said to be really educated. For this sort of education there is demanded*

---

[25] UNESCO (1997) *Environment and Society: Education and public awareness for sustainability,* Background Paper prepared for UNESCO International Conference, Thessaloniki,.

rigorous discipline of the powers of observation, of the reason, and especially of the will."
- William Congreve

As humans we get education from our own or from the experiences of others (through formal and informal schooling).

The uniqueness of Education as a key driver for transformation is that it conveys good thoughts, beautiful ideology and philosophical concept about life and the human race. These thoughts have been preserved in various forms, such as books and are readily transfer to upcoming generations via schooling.

Life is a journey and education is one of the ways you get acquainted with life and all that it entails. So education in its simplest form means learning life lessons.

When education thoroughly permeates an individual, it carries the person in the way of success and fulfillment. With education, an individual learns to use the brain for making decisions and creating pathways that will enhance his or her survival and enables him or her to gain relevance on earth.

At the end of schooling and the acquisition of knowledge, a certificate is normally awarded as a proof of school attendance and not an evidence of knowledge acquisition.

Wake up! Take This Job!

The proof that I attended University of Benin, Benin City is that I have a degree which is symbolized by a paper certificate. But the evidence that I gained knowledge in University is manifested in how I deal with the various challenges that life hurls at me. One of such life challenges is getting a job after graduation.

If your certificate cannot get you a job, what will you fall back to? If you have an education, you could put your brain to work. But a situation where you got your certificate without an education and paper qualification without the development of your personality, you will have nothing to fall back to.

You will join those shouting that there is no job; you will blame everyone, from the government to your family members for your predicament.

> The truth is that you were never sent to school to get a certificate, you were sent to get an education, to acquire knowledge that will enable you to survive.

The truth is that you were never sent to school to get a certificate, you were sent to get an education and to acquire knowledge that will enable you to survive and gain relevance on earth. Certificate is only a proof that you attended school.

It is like marriage. You will agree with me that the marriage certificate is not marriage; it is just a proof that two people are married. Imagine a scenario where the marriage registry issued out marriage certificate to an individual who has no spouse? And the person concerned goes into town brandishing the certificate of marriage and when asked about his spouse, he is looks surprised as he has no wife in the first place.

This is exactly what has happened to majority of our youth; we graduated with certificates, but without an education. We have good paper qualifications without the development of our personality. We have good grades, but lack the ability to trade.

When we are asked about our education, we are dumbfounded; we have nothing to show, because we never had it in the first place. You cannot give what you do not have.

THE KIND OF EDUCATION THAT WE NEED

The kind of education that we need in Nigeria is business education. Udonkang gave a very sound definition of what education should be in his work *"Comparative Studies of Business Education and other Discipline in Nigeria*[26]*"*

He defines Business Education as "***a programme of vocational training designed to equip students with the knowledge, skills and attitudes that are essential for gainful employment so that the students may learn to live as useful and acceptable members of their communities***".

Oladunjoye also gave a similar but more concise definition of the subject in his book *"The principle of Business Studies"* He defined Business Education as "***a type of education or training for preparing the individual for the world of work***".

Broken down, business education which is a subset of the general education can be seen as the development of a person's head, heart and hands for his self-sustenance, fulfillment and optimum services to humanity. If every youth is empowered with such

---

[26] Udon Kang E.C. (2002) Comparative Studies of Business Education and other Discipline in Nigeria *Ekpo Educational Journal.* Vol. 7, No. 10, Pg 6-7

utilitarian education, I do not think the unemployment rate will be as high as it is presently.

REVENUE GENERATION AND EDUCATION

Education is the primary agent of transformation and the vehicle that can transport individuals as well as communities to a better future; because it increases people's capacities to transform their life visions and that of the society that they live in into practical reality.

Education does not end in the laboratory and classrooms, and it does not only provide scientific and technical skills. But also provides the drive and necessary support for pursuing and applying acquired knowledge for the benefit of society.

For this very reason, every aspect of our society must be deeply concerned that much of current education falls far short of what is expected.

All hands must be on deck to preserve the future of our children and that of unborn generation from decadence. This can be achieved through a concerted effort at improving the standard of education.

Improving the standard, quality and means of conveying education and reorienting the appropriate authorities, teachers as well as students to recognize the importance of revenue generation after acquisition of education must be among our highest priorities.

Revenue generation places a demand on the knowledge you have acquired on the platform of education. This knowledge is in the form of workable skills. Even if you get a good job, your certificate is only a gate pass; after you get the job a demand will be placed on your knowledge.

Nobody pays you for your certificate, you are paid for the problem you solve with the knowledge you have acquired.

Success begins the moment you understand that life pays you for the problem you solve with the education or the skills that you have acquired. This is what I call "purposeful education".

Start solving problems, start doing something worthwhile with what you have. Opportunities are always where you are. Use what you have to create what you desire.

LIFE PRINCIPLES FROM CHAPTER SEVEN

- *The strategy for you to generate income is not solely based on your certificate, but on the education you have acquired.*
- *Paper qualification is at war with personality development.*
- *Education is the totality of life experience that man acquires which enables him to cope with and derive satisfaction from living in the world.*
- *Education "is supposed to prepare an individual for a career in life. Unfortunately, most Nigerian children go into various stages of education, right from the primary to tertiary institutions without any preparation for whatever career stages they aim at".*
- *The truth is that you were never sent to school to get a certificate, you were sent to get an education, to acquire knowledge that will enable you to survive.*
- *Revenue generation places a demand on the knowledge you have acquired on the platform of education*
- *Success begins the moment you understand that life pays you for the problem you solve with the education or the skills that you have acquired.*

CHAPTER

8

"The longer you are not taking action the more money you are losing"

– Carrie Wilkerson

CHAPTER EIGHT

STEPPING IN AS AN ENTREPRENEUR

"If you cannot risk, you cannot grow"
– David Viscott

One of the best educations that guarantee financial independence is entrepreneurial education. It is the education for self-sustenance and self-reliance. To be frank it took me a while to begin to appreciate the importance of entrepreneurial education.

While in the University, we were introduced to a course titled: Entrepreneurship (CED 300). I really did not pay serious attention to it; I had to read and pass it because it was a mandatory course. But, after NYSC, I brought out the text book: **"Entrepreneurship Development: the Nigerian Experience"**[27] and began to devour it. I read it from cover to cover, until I grasped the concept in its totality.

That book was very helpful and useful to me as it gave me the necessary information I needed to stay afloat after NYSC. I really appreciate the effort of Prof. MacOliver and his team for putting that wonderful book together. My only regret is that, I did not start reading it

---

[27] MacOliver F.O. *et al* (2000) Entrepreneurship **Development: The Nigerian Experience.** Mareh Publishers, Benin City

on time. I strongly recommend that book to all graduates.

The other day I was reading **First Bank Review**[28], where 'Tunde Popoola wrote about "*The Job Creation Imperative*" he said that "mass unemployment in Nigeria can be tackled by formulating economic policies and programmes that will encourage entrepreneurship, self-employment and improvement in labour productivity ..."

In the absence of high profile and high wage jobs, young men and women, now have no choice but to opt for self-employment which is another name for entrepreneurship. But who is an entrepreneur?

Collins Concise English Dictionary defines an entrepreneur as ***"the owner or manager of a business enterprise who, by risks and initiative, attempts to make profits"***.

Robert Kiyosaki in his book **"Retire Young, Retire Rich**[29]**"** defines an entrepreneur as someone that sees an opportunity, put together a team, and builds a business that profit from the opportunity." He also defines a tradesman or a craftsman as someone who can produce a product or provide a service primarily by himself.

> An entrepreneur is "the owner or manager of a business enterprise who, by risks and initiative, attempts to make profits"

---

[28] Popoola A.T. (2012) The Job Creation Imperative. *First Bank Review A Semi-Annual Journal of Business and the Economy*" Vol. 2. Is.1.Pg 34.

[29] Kiyosaki, Robert (1999) **Retire Young, Retire Rich**. New York, Warner Books.

An entrepreneur is described as a person who starts a new business, he is a venture capitalist, has a high level of achievement, motivation and is either naturally endowed or has acquired the qualities of enthusiasm, idealism, sense of purpose and independence of thought and action.

An entrepreneur after starting business, organizes other factors of production, develops and introduces new products, raises the necessary funds and risks failure and loss of investment against the chance of earning a profit.

Entrepreneurship on the other hand is defined as the willingness and ability of an individual to seek out investment opportunities, establish and run an enterprise successfully.

WHY RISK BEING AN ENTREPRENEUR

The desire to make money is one of the driving forces behind entrepreneurship; but starting your own business can be scaring and thrilling at the same time.

Apart from making money, people take the risk of starting their own business because of the following reasons.

i. Opportunity – to put in the best for one self.
ii. Profit – the reward for taking risk
iii. Independence - they do not enjoy working for others
iv. Joy of achievement –the joy of taking risk and succeeding to achieve your goal
v. Job security- nobody can sack you. There is no such thing as downsizing.
vi. A better alternative to an endless search for job

Wake up! Take This Job!

Anyone with a strong will can become an entrepreneur.

The scripture says

> **"The kingdom of God is within you"**
> -Luke 17:21

What this means is that you have what it takes to become anything that is within the kingdom of God. One of such thing in the kingdom is called entrepreneurship. Entrepreneurship is not just an economic concept; it is a biblical pattern of living.

For example, the patriarchs were all great farmers, Abraham was rich in cattle, and Isaac was established in the cattle business and so were Jacob and his descendants.

To prove further that God does not tolerate laziness, idleness and a wait-to-be-fed attitude, He stopped sending manna from heaven the moment the children of Israel stepped foot into the Promised Land. God expected then to work.

> *You do not have to be a genius, an inventor, or posses any extraordinary ability.*

Even Jesus Christ was an entrepreneur; scripture described him as a carpenter.

> **"Is not this the carpenter, the son of Mary...?"**
> -Mark 6:3

He had a vocational skill with which he generated income for himself.

If Jesus was engaged in entrepreneurship in spite of the fact of His divine origin, I do not think any person out

Wake up! Take This Job!

there has any reason why he or she should not engage in entrepreneurial pursuits.

To be an entrepreneur, you do not have to be a genius, an inventor, or posses any extraordinary ability. All you need is some basic knowledge about what you want to do, how you can go about it and the fortitude to take the first step and start doing what you want to do.

SEVEN RULES OF ENGAGEMENT FOR AN UPCOMING ENTREPRENEUR

"If one does not know to which port one is sailing, no wind is favorable."
-Lucius Seneca

In stepping into the arena of business as a young entrepreneur and establishing your own business, there are seven fundamental rules that should be observed. If followed, an individual may become successful in his or her entrepreneurial pursuit.

RULE #ONE
KNOW WHAT TO DO

This speaks of a clear cut vision of what you are out to do. It speaks of the idea, the products or services you intend to render. Until what to do is discovered, nothing can be done. You cannot go to the market without a product to sell.

RULE #TWO
KNOW HOW TO DO IT

Knowing what to do is the easiest part, but knowing how to go about it might be a herculean task. This speaks of strategy, it include a detailed plan on how you intend to transform your vision or idea into practical reality. It involves setting goal and formulating plans to achieve them.

RULE #THREE
KNOW WHEN TO DO IT

The difference between 99^0c and 100^0 c is just 1 degree and that 1 degree makes a big difference between steaming and boiling water. The interval between 99^0c and 100^0c degree could be a split second; that split seconds is crucial to the boiling point of water. Timing is crucial to success, when the right thing is done at the right time, success is guaranteed. Knowing when to do what we intend to do speaks of programming; a programme is a deliberate schedule of what to do and when to do it.

RULE # FOUR
WHERE TO DO IT

There is a location for every event or business on earth. You cannot be doing a fishing business in the desert; fish cannot be caught in the desert. If you site your business in the wrong location, you might not make the kind of progress you desire. Environment and habitat, is the place where people or animals live, if you want to attend to a particular group of people, you need to go where they live.

RULE # FIVE
WHO TO DO IT

Things don't just happen by chance, people make things happen. But not all people can make things happen for you. Mary Kay Ash says that *"there are three categories of people on earth: those who make things happen; those who watch things happen and those who wonder about what is happening"*. If you enlist the right set of people, you will definitely get the right set of result. Who to do it also speaks of the persons whose input is required to get the job done.

RULE # SIX
WHAT TOOL(S) TO USE

There are different tools for different jobs. You cannot use a screw driver to do the work of a spanner. There are certain skills that are needed for certain jobs, if you lack the skill there is no way you can get the job done, except you employ someone with the skill that you lack. What tools to use also entails the amount of money that is needed to realise your dream, financial planning is crucial to success in any endeavour. It also means the technical know-how that is needed to get the job done. For you to succeed in certain venture, you may need to undergo some training to get the skills that are relevant to that venture.

RULE # SEVEN
WHERE TO SELL IT AND WHO TO BUY IT

For a product to bring profit there must be a buyer. A product without a target market will forever remain in the custody of the maker. In fact, rule number seven is fundamental to every other rule. You must decide the end user of your product or services, before you start production. If you are writing a book, for instance, who are the people you expect to read your book. A product with a specific target will definitely sell.

SEVEN INDISPENSABLE QUALITIES OF A SUCCESSFUL ENTREPRENEUR

Research has shown that there are certain personal characteristics and qualities usually peculiar to successful entrepreneurs. I refer to these qualities as **the entrepreneurial attitude.**

While some people are of the opinion that these attitudes are innate, I believe they can be acquired by learning.

Wake up! Take This Job!

Park In his book, **How to succeed in your own business**[30], identified some traits that a successful entrepreneur should possess.

i. **INITIATIVE:** successful entrepreneur are original, skilful, resourceful and quick to embrace opportunities. Initiative is the personal ability of starting an action. It involves being able to act without prompting.

ii. **ATTITUDE:** successful entrepreneurs have positive mental attitude and are usually warm to people, exhibiting good disposition to win friendships. They are very receptive. They nurture and protect those relationship connected to their dreams.

iii. **LEADERSHIP:** successful entrepreneurs are good leaders who greatly inspire people and by so doing earn high loyalty. Great leaders inspire people to go places or do things they would never have thought of on their own. They assert a lot of influence among their workers and business associates.

iv. **DECISIVENESS:** successful entrepreneurs are usually decisive, they respond promptly and accurately each time decisions are to be made. Indecision or delayed decision can be detrimental to a business initiator, thus the need for good mental alertness at all times. It is better to make a wrong decision, rather than not making any decision.

v. **PERSEVERANCE**: To be named a successful entrepreneur means that you have to persevere till

---

[30] Park, W.R and Park S.C.(1978) **How to succeed in your business,** Chichester, John Wiley and Sons.

you realise you dream. Successful entrepreneurs do not give up. Giving up is not an option. A teabag will not release its flavour until it goes through hot water. Successful people never quit. Their slogan is: I will persist till I succeed.

vi. **SELF DISCIPLINE**: successful entrepreneurs are self disciplined. They subject themselves to rules and laws in order to achieve their ultimate goals in life.

vii. **FEARLESS AND BOLD:** successful entrepreneur are bold and fearless, they are not intimidated by anything. Even when they are afraid, they still make moves that showcase courage and strength.

THE SYNERGY BETWEEN SKILLS ACQUISITION AND ENTREPRENEURSHIP

If your desire to be economically self-reliant will ever see the light of the day, then you must of a necessity embrace the concept of acquiring new skills. Each time an opportunity arise for you to get a new skill, I strongly suggest that you grab it.

According to Encarta Dictionary (2009), a skill is seen as ability to do something well, usually gained through training or experience. Skill acquisition on the other hand involves the development of a new skill, practice or a way of doing things usually gained through training or experience.

Concerning the world of business, Jennifer Aniston once made the following assertions:

Wake up! Take This Job!

"I was told to avoid the business all together because of the rejection. People would say to me, 'Don't you want to have a normal job and a normal family?' I guess that would be good advice for some people, but I wanted to act."

In today's Nigeria, the quickest way to economic freedom is the utilization of skill and the ability to act on what you know. Like we said earlier, certificate may not give you what you long for, but skill will never disappoint you. A man with skill will never go hungry.

> An educated mind is a fertile ground for ideas to germinate.

From ancient times, human beings have been striving to master and improve their environment. This quest has continually increased the need for acquiring new relevant skills.

It is a well-known fact that effective training in skill acquisition has immensely contributed to the technological excellence and economic self-reliance of the industrialized nations.

> In today's Nigeria, the quickest way to economic freedom is the utilization of skill.

Skill acquisition and development has been man's means of material transformation. It is only with skilled men that materials can be harnessed, manipulated and transformed into products.

There are countless of examples of the transformation of materials into more useful products:

Wake up! Take This Job!

What is the difference between a timber in the forest and the furniture in your living room? The furniture in your living room contains the same materials as the log of wood in the forest. The difference is that the furniture has gone through the workmanship of a skilled furniture maker.

It has become more valuable than it was in its raw state. The price of the furniture cannot be compare to the price of the timber. The furniture could be 10, 20, 30, 40 or even 50 times the price of the timber. This shows that skills are at the foundation of the transformation of materials.

Another example is crude oil. For many years, the Niger Delta sat on billions of barrels of crude oil and several billion of gas without knowing, until the men with the appropriate skills showed up. Today several billions of barrels of crude oil are being exported to Europe and America where they are refined and brought back to Nigeria and resold to us at almost 100 times the price.

No matter who you are, what you have, where you live or the educational qualifications that you may possess, if you want to be relevant in today's Nigeria, you need to acquire some new skills. Your degree is no longer enough.

I have met degree holders from different fields who are not relevant in their area of qualification. You must go beyond certification; paper qualification is no longer enough. Skills are the in-thing today.

If you are a graduate and you are hunting for a job there is no certainty that anybody is going to offer you a job. The onus is on you to find the employment

Wake up! Take This Job!

opportunities that are out there or, in some cases to create your own. This is a new role for most people, and our education, training and in some cases our upbringing does not prepare us well for it.

Acquiring self-reliance skills is not only necessary, but crucial to your survival.

Emphasising the importance of self-reliance and skill acquisition to job seekers, Nigeria's former Vice President, Atiku Abubakar urged the poor and unemployed population to begin to appreciate the option of being self-reliant rather than waiting for government patronage.

He stated that *"we cannot just sit back in our homes and imagine that because we have acquired some education, nothing more is required of us... equipped with that education, we should learn to use our hands and to produce. This is the best solution to the problem of poverty and unemployment"*.[31]

MONETIZE YOUR IDEA AND SKILLS

An educated mind is a fertile ground for ideas to germinate. Revenue is generated when ideas are monetised. The crystallised form of idea is money. Ideas are crystallised when they are converted to money. Idea is often abstract and intangible.

The evidence that an idea works is determined by the amount of money it produces or the number of people it impacts. If you have an education, then you will definitely have an idea, if you have an idea, you can turn your idea to money. An idea that cannot be

---

[31] Quoted by Hon. Joseph Gumbari *The Importance Of Skills Acquisition* "The National Assembly Legislative Digest" Vol 2:
http://www.nasslegisdigestonline.com/newsdesc.php?id=134

converted into its monetary equivalent is not idea; it is just a dream.

THE MIDAS TOUCH

There is this story about a king in ancient Greece called King Midas. King Midas was a very kind man who ruled his kingdom fairly, but he was not one to think very deeply about what he said.

One day, while walking in his garden, he saw an elderly satyr asleep in the flowers. Taking pity on the old fellow, King Midas let him go without punishment. When the god Dionysus heard about it, he rewarded King Midas by granting him one wish.

The king thought for only a second and then said I wish for everything I touch to turn to gold." And so it was.

The beautiful flowers in his garden turned toward the sun for light, but when Midas approached and touched them, they

> Until you reach out for something, it always remains the way it is. Things don't just happen, people make things to happen.

became rigid and golden. The king grew hungry and thin, for each time he tried to eat, he found that his meal had turned to gold. His lovely daughter, at his loving touch, turned hard and fast to gold. His water, his bed, his clothes, his friends, and eventually the whole palace was gold.

King Midas saw that soon his whole kingdom would turn to gold unless he did something right away. He asked Dionysus to turn everything back to the way it had been and take back his golden touch. Because the king was ashamed and very sad, Dionysus took pity on him and granted his request. Instantly, everything changed back to normal, but the king felt richer, in the things that really count.

There are so many interpretations and moral lessons to this story. The point I want us to see is that **only the things that King Midas touched changed to gold. Whatever he refuse to touch remain the way it was.**

Until you reach out for something, it always remains the way it is. Things do not just happen, people make things to happen. This is in consonance with Newton's first law of motion which states that: **every object will remain in its state of rest until a force is applied to it.**

You have to reach down inside you and draw out the skills and education that you have to change your world.

> *"Put your knowledge to action to enable you impact positively on yourself and society at large"*
> -E.E.Ukeredi

THE HARD WAY, THE BEST WAY

Make no mistake: Entrepreneurship is not an easy option for anybody most especially for a fresh graduate. It is best suited for those with the necessary skills and acumen.

The truth is that for every individual who succeeds in a new business venture, there are hundreds (maybe even thousands) who fail. Why? Because there is much more to entrepreneurship and being self-employed than wearing suit and tie.

Being a successful entrepreneur requires some real-life information, a business owner skill set, a significant tolerance for risk, and most importantly, an entrepreneurial attitude.

If you decide to start your own business, you are likely to experience some problems. Many of these problems apply to anyone starting a new enterprise but some problems are related to the youthful age of the entrepreneur.

As a youth, you are likely to have limited business knowledge, networks and contacts compared with older people.

You are also likely to have fewer financial resources at your disposal as you have had less time to accumulate personal savings or acquire property. You are also like to be mistrusted.

You may experience age discrimination from clients, suppliers or finance lenders.[32]
As hard as it may seem, it is by far the best path to follow in the time that we live in.

To wind up this chapter, let us consider one of the richest men on earth: Bill Gate, that Bill is a Harvard drop out is not news, that he is among the richest men on earth is not news, what we often overlook is that as at the time he left Harvard he was not awarded a degree. He left Harvard without a certificate but he had an education. His education created Microsoft Corporation and today the evidence of that education is obvious.
Demand was placed on the knowledge he has acquired and the result is glaring.

You must push yourself out of the crowd of those who had certificate without knowledge. You must put a demand on the knowledge that you have, no matter how little that knowledge is.

---

[32] Kenyon, P. and White, S. (2001): *Enterprise-Based Youth Employment Policies, Strategies and Programmes,* International Labour Office, Geneva, p. 7

Wake up! Take This Job!

Once you begin to place a demand on the knowledge you have, your perception of unemployment will change, you will begin to see things differently, you will see that not having a job is not a disadvantage, it is actually an advantage in disguise. As soon as this reality dawns on you, your life will take a different dimension.

"Remember that what you take for granted because it is a common knowledge to you, is a revelation, a secret of immense value to someone who does not know or understand it. Do not undervalue what you know"

LIFE PRINCIPLES FROM CHAPTER EIGHT

- *An entrepreneur is "the owner or manager of a business enterprise who, by risks and initiative, attempts to make profits"*

- *You do not have to be a genius, an inventor, or possess any extraordinary ability to be an entrepreneur.*

- *In today's Nigeria, the quickest way to economic freedom is the utilization of skill.*

- *Acquiring self-reliance skills is not only necessary, but crucial to your survival.*

- *An educated mind is a fertile ground for ideas to germinate. Revenue is generated when ideas are monetized.*

- *Until you reach out for something, it always remains the way it is. Things do not just happen, people make things to happen.*

CHAPTER

9

"Many people see technology as the problem behind the so-called digital divide. Others see it as the solution. Technology is neither. It must operate in conjunction with business, economic, political and social system."

-Carly Fiorina

CHAPTER NINE

THE DIGITAL SHIFT

"My own experience is use the tools that are out there. Use the digital world..."
-Colin Powell

In the 20th Century, an educated person was he who could read and write. Now with the advent, advancement and development in technology particularly with information and communication technology in the 21st century, the definition of an educated person has changed to those who can read, write and at the same time are equipped with the indispensable ICT skill of being computer literate.

The world is shrinking, what seemed so vast and unreachable is now within our reach. ICT has reduced the world into a global village and the complexity of acquiring education is no longer achievable only under the four-walls of a classroom but at the finger tips, at the click of a computer mouse.

> Our future does not depend on oil and gas but on the quality of human capital.

The most practical skill that has helped me thus far in life is ICT skill. In fact, it was pivotal to my ability to weather the storm of unemployment. Life would have been hard, if not unbearable for me but for the ICT skill I acquired early in my University days. I can boldly say that ninety percent of the things that bring money to me are ICT related

OUR FUTURE, OUR TOMORROW

I want you to know that our future does not depend on oil and gas but on the quality of our human capital. In this digital age, Nigeria needs quality manpower. We must get our priorities right by investing seriously in human capital development.

This means focusing on increased computer literacy and ICT professionalism. The level of IT literacy is still abysmally low due to grinding poverty in the land and ignorance.

Now is the time to prepare the populace, by growing their IT skills for the knowledge economy. Although this book is not an ICT book, I think it is necessary for us to have some knowledge of the fundamental concept of ICT.

UNDERSTANDING ICT

If we accept the notion that ICT has a potential for the development and that the future depends on choices made in our society today, then one must try to grasp what impact ICT will have on development both for individuals as well as institutions. But first of all, we must understand what ICT is.

WHAT IS ICT?

ICT is an acronym for information and communication Technology but beyond this acronym, there is not a universally accepted definition of ICT. Why? Because the concepts, methods and applications involved in ICT are constantly evolving almost on daily basis. It is difficult to keep up with the changes – they happen so fast-A good way to think about ICT is to consider all the uses

> Information and communication technologies are the tools that underpin the emerging "information society."

of digital technology that already exist to help individuals, businesses and organisations use information.

ICT covers any product that will store, retrieve, manipulate, transmits or receives information electronically in a digital form. For example, personal computer, digital television, email, robots. [33]

Information and Communication Technology (ICT) ***is an umbrella term that includes computer hardware and software, digital broadcast and telecommunications technologies as well as digital information repositories online or offline.***[34]

And it includes contemporary social networking aspects, read/write interfaces on the web besides file sharing systems online. It represents a broad and continually evolving range of elements that further includes the television (TV), radio, mobile phones and the policies and laws that govern the widespread use of these media and devices. *(Selwyn, 2002),*

Information and communication technologies are the tools that underpin the emerging *"information society."*

Information exchange between people and through networks of people has always taken place. The ICT

---

[33] www.tutor24.net.2006
[34] Selwyn, N. 2002, *Defining the 'Digital Divide':* developing a theoretical understanding of inequalities in the information age.
Available at: http://www.cf.ac.uk/socsi/ict/definingdigitaldivide.pdf

enablement of information exchange, however, has radically changed the magnitude of this exchange, and thus, factors such as timeliness of information and information dissemination patterns have become more important than ever.

Another term commonly used to describe the changes produced by information technology is the *"digital divide"*, a term which refers to the gap between those who benefit from digital technology and those who do not.

ICT REVOLUTION AND YOU
"While technology shapes the future, it is people who shape technology and decide what it can and should be used for"
- Kofi Annan

Whether you are eight or eighty years old, you need ICT. But young people need it more than any other category, Youth population is exploding, yet young people have too often been seen as a burden rather than an asset, a group to be taught but not to teach, and to receive but not to give.

Youth need to be engaged in decision-making processes related to the information society - as students, and as citizens with an affinity for technology, they are informed stakeholders in the evolution of education and innovation.

As a youth, you need ICT more than any other person in the world today. Because, with ICT knowledge you could become one of the key drivers of today's economy. It is therefore, important for you to get acquainted with the trends in the ICT world; refusal to get acquainted could land you in obscurity and oblivion.

Wake up! Take This Job!

It is no longer news that we live in a world driven and powered by intellect and technology, a world where we see a nation rise and fall as a result of its embrace or neglect of information and communication technology. Your relevance is tied to ICT knowledge. Ignore ICT at your peril.

EMBRACING THE ICT REVOLUTION FOR SELF EMPOWERMENT

According to the World Bank[35],

> *"Information is a critical ingredient for development. The more information that the poor possess, the greater their sense of empowerment. Empowered citizens can more readily hold governments accountable. With greater information the poor also are better able to organize and take actions to improve their quality of life."*

With the advent of network technology such as the Internet and the World Wide Web, the face of human interaction has changed. In some cases, it has become bigger and more expansive, where the potential for knowledge exchange is tremendous.

Where previously, two young people from around the world would never have met, Internet and Communications Technologies such as social networks (Facebook, Twitter), social media networks (Idealist, TakingITGlobal), and digital media platforms (YouTube, MySpace and the Youth Media Exchange Project), have aided an

> *ICT knowledge has being acknowledged globally as a panacea to unemployment problem among youth.*

---

[35] Available at: *web.worldbank.org / e-Government /Knowledge Resource*

Wake up! Take This Job!

unprecedented level of interaction between individuals, communities and entire regions across the world. The potential for empowerment in such interactions is vast, especially where youth are concerned.

Youth unemployment as pointed out earlier in this book has become one of the biggest developmental challenges in this country. So far, efforts by governments to promote job creation through planned programmes, both in the private and public sectors have been ad-hoc and insufficient.

Apart from the difficulty of getting a job in this country, there is growing pressure on young graduates to compete in an increasingly globalised labour market.

Furthermore, the impact of globalisation in terms of opening up markets for the youth in Nigeria has been non-existent or negligible in most cases, contributing further to widening the gap between the rich and the poor, and the skilled and the unskilled.

Empowerment is about skills and capacity building to be productive and as such a crucial aspect of the empowerment goal is the acquisition of relevant technological skills. ICT knowledge has been acknowledged globally as a panacea to unemployment problem among youth.

You just have to step into the popular *"Robson Plaza"* in Warri, to appreciate the impact of ICT for youth empowerment. Within the plaza you will see hundreds of young people fully engaged in one form of ICT related job or the other, this range from phone repairs and configuration to laptop repairs, software sales and installations.

Wake up! Take This Job!

In fact, if you have a problem with your computer or your mobile phones and you live in Warri, the best place to visit is the *"Plaza."* If you cannot resolve you ICT problem in the *"Plaza"*, you will get a good reference that will be very useful to you.

Jobs in the ICT industry are not only for computer science and engineering graduates, but for as many as are willing to take their destiny into their hands and acquire new relevant skills.

The unalloyed truth is that as a youth, without ICT skill you will be irrelevant in the scheme of things. It is either you brace up to take the bold step of acquiring ICT knowledge or live the rest of your life at the bottom of the food chain. ICT knowledge is more than browsing the Internet, face booking and pinging on blackberry.

ICT is an enabler and also a driver of development in any nation especially in the present day economy; it is one sector that impacts on every other sector. It can be put clearly that no sector will grow to its full potential in our world today without using ICT, be it Finance, Agriculture, Education, Entertainment, Health and even the Church.

> *Whether you are eight or eighty years old, you need ICT.*

And no nation will ever become relevant among the comity of nations in the present economies if this key driver is not taken seriously. If all you have is ICT knowledge, you are equipped enough to gain relevance. With your ICT skill you will soon discover that your services are needed by someone out there.

BRIDGING THE DIGITAL DIVIDE

Wake up! Take This Job!

The development of the Information and Knowledge Society shows outstanding differences between individuals, places, cities, countries and regions, thus leading to the existence of the so called digital divide. The difference between a graduate, who landed a job with a multinational company and another graduate with better grades but who could not get a good job, might just be as a result of ICT knowledge.

While the number of educated youth continues to grow nationwide, there is insufficient knowledge about the use of ICT among graduates, and the role that ICT-based skills has in terms of future employment opportunities.

Some graduates do not even have email addresses; some are even alien to the concept of Facebook. In this age of online application for jobs, I wonder how such people will survive. I have met graduates who claimed to have attended computer schools, yet they cannot differentiate between hardware and software. Some even have computers but cannot operate them. This is very disturbing.

I once met a secondary school teacher who teaches computer science, but without a practical knowledge of the computer, all she knows is theory. Yet she goes to the classroom everyday to theorize a practical subject. If the teacher does not know, how will the student learn? We are not talking about people in the rural area, I mean in the city, among so called enlightened people. If the teacher does not know, how will the student learn?

> The truth is that as a youth, without ICT skill you will be irrelevant in the scheme of things.

The information and communication technology (ICT) gap is enormous.

The gap exists *"between developed and developing countries. A person in a high-income country is over 22 times more likely to be an Internet user than someone in a low-income country. Secure Internet servers, a rough indicator of electronic commerce, are over 100 times more common in high-income than in low-income countries. In high-income countries, mobile phones are 29 times more prevalent and mainline penetration is 21 times that of low-income countries. Relative to income, the cost of Internet access in a low-income country is 150 times the cost of a comparable service in a high income country. There are similar divides within individual countries. ICT is often non-existent in poor and rural areas of developing countries...[36]"*

As a young person with boundless energy, imagination, creativity, ideas, and a limitless vision, your dreams can easily manifest if you can bridge the current digital divide that separates you from the rest of the world. If you fail to bridge this gap your future and that of the society in which you live might be compromised.

A youth that is equipped with sound ICT knowledge could be a key agent for social change, economic development and technological innovation.

One of your goals as a young person should be to narrow the digital divide. This can be done through
• Learning and acquiring ICT education,

- Active participation in ICT related activities in and around you, activities such as multimedia, social networking like Facebook, Tweeter etc.

---

[36] United Nations Conference on Trade and Development (2005) The digital divide report: ICT diffusion index.
http://unctad.org/en/Docs/iteipc20065_en.pdf

- Openness to learn and use new technology as they are unfolding

The use of information and communication technologies (ICT) is skyrocketing. You must be resilient in the acquisition of ICT-driven skills. Let us see some of the benefits of ICT.

SEIZING THE BENEFITS OF ICT IN A DIGITAL ECONOMY

ICT helps you connect, collaborate and compete effectively. A strong ICT (information and communications technology) knowledge base is pivotal to competitive survival for today's world.

It has become a pervasive part of our working and living environments, and will continue to be an integral resource for business, government and society at large. It is the key to helping individuals and organisations of all sizes to connect, collaborate and compete more effectively. Some benefits of ICT are listed below.

i. Enhance Your Employability

ICT skills are not just required for jobs in the information technology (IT) sector. The demand for ICT skills cuts across every sector and job type. ICT skills are increasingly important in sectors such as agriculture, construction, education and service industries. In today's labour market, ICT-related occupations represent an important slice of economic activity.

ii. E-Learning

The "e-learning" term is a general term used to refer to computer-enhanced learning. It is used interchangeably in so many contexts that it is critical to be clear what one means when one speaks of "e-Learning". In many respects, it is commonly associated with the field of Advanced Learning Technology (ALT), which deals with both the technologies and associated methodologies in learning using networked and/or multimedia technologies.

ICT provides:
- free access to the best and biggest libraries in the world
- vast, endless world of information at your fingertips
- online academic programmes (diplomas; degrees, certifications, etc)

iii. Access To Business: the internet provide a very good platform to access business opportunities. There are number of websites that contain useful publications for business development. With the internet you can do business with different people across the globe.

iv. Communication: ICT-based interaction between young people is common. Communication between friends and strangers may occur using real names or pseudonyms (virtual personalities or net identities), or anonymously.
- keeps you in touch with diverse opportunities
- links you with people of all races and eliminates distance and geographical boundaries

v. Job Creation: ICT has the inherent potential for job creation, it expands your horizon and reach for employment, it grants you 'global citizenship' Innovation/wealth creation and an endless opportunity to break new grounds and create job for yourself and others.

vi. *ICT bridge the gap between the rich and the poor*: ICTs help to bridge the gap between the rich and the poor. ICT does not discriminate. Whether you are rich or poor, as long as you have the skill you can enjoy the benefit.

Now that you know the importance of ICT, it is time to get to work.

LIFE PRINCIPLES FROM CHAPTER NINE

- *Our future as a people does not depend on oil and gas but on the quality of human capital.*
- *Information and communication technologies are the tools that underpin the emerging "information society."*
- *Whether you are eight or eighty years old, you need ICT*
- *The truth is that as a youth without ICT skill you will be irrelevant in the scheme of things.*
- *ICT helps you connect collaborate and compete effectively.*

CHAPTER

10

"Will power is the key to success. Successful people strive no matter what they feel by applying their will to overcome apathy, doubt or fear."

-Dan Millman

CHAPTER TEN

DEALING WITH IMMOBILIZERS

According to Zig Ziglar in his book *"Top Performance*[37]*"*. He said that there are three great immobilizers that keep people from succeeding. The immobilizers are FEAR, DOUBT AND WORRY. I completely believe what he said.

These are the tripartite enemies of a fresh graduate. They are so interrelated that wherever you find one, you will definitely see the others. Their effect could be so strong to the extent that they could paralyze even the most brilliant person. But we shall learn in this chapter how to deal with them and gain a decisive victory.

Once the immobilizers are dealt with, you can take your journey to the zenith and nothing will hold you back.

All that has been said so far in this book will be meaningless if you cannot conquer Fear, Doubt and Worry (FDW).

DEALING WITH F.E.A.R

(Fear means False Evidence Appearing Real.)

Nothing in life is to be feared, it is only to be understood.
-Marie Curie

---

[37] Zig Ziglar (1986) *Top Performance*, New York The Berkley Publishing Group.

First and foremost, understand that you always have a choice about how to respond to and deal with fear. You can cave in to it, struggle with it, accept it, or work around it. You always have a choice, a choice you can make again and again or that you can change based on your assessment of what is best for you.

> The more information you have the less doubt you will feel.

Hear what John C. Maxwell has to say about what fear can create in a person's life.

- Fear breeds in action
- Inaction breeds lack of experience
- Lack of experience breeds ignorance
- Ignorance breeds fear

DEALING WITH FEAR

Make a list of all of your fears, include every fear, however small or irrational then read them aloud to yourself.

The next thing to do is to acquire relevant knowledge about the things you are afraid of. Knowledge is light and fear is darkness, light always prevails over darkness.

For instance, if you are not adequately prepared for an examination, you are likely to have fear. Because you lack adequate knowledge about what is ahead, but if you a well prepared, you exude confidence.

Once you know your fears, attack them with prayer. Fear always bows to superior power. Prayer can extinguish fear, just as water can extinguish fire. The fire of fear will be quenched by a heartfelt prayer. Prayer instills unusual confidence and faith toward God.

I have personally discovered that whenever I pray about something that frightens me, an unusual boldness and courage to confront it suddenly engulfs me. Never underestimate the power of prayer in dealing with fear.

The next thing to do is to confront your fear. If you are afraid of water, take a swimming class. If you are afraid of snakes; visit a zoo where there are snakes.

If you shy away from talking to people because you fear that your level of ignorance might be revealed; then join a teaching club or Sunday Teacher's forum, which provides an avenue for you to defeat your fear.

The lesson here is that when you run away from your fear, you will meet it in front of you. The best thing to do is to face your fear. Your fear cannot stand you. You have power over anything that scares you. When you run away from your fear, it grows bigger the next time you see it. But every time you face your worst fear, it gets smaller and smaller in size.

DEALING WITH DOUBT
"Our doubts are traitors, and make us lose the good we often might win, by fearing to attempt"
-William Shakespeare

We all have doubts; it is part of being human. Depending on how you deal with them, they can guide you away from potentially difficult/dangerous situations or cause you to miss many great opportunities.

Doubts creep into our minds and are capable of doing a lot of damage. It is important we learn to understand why we get them and what purpose they serve us under each situation.

For instance, I had doubts about writing this book. My doubts like most others arose in the form of questions: "will this book be finished?" "Will people appreciate it?" I have come to trust my doubts as they usually lead me to be more proactive and creative. I have learned not to allow my doubt stop me from doing what I know I should do.

No matter how positive and convinced we are, sometimes, doubt creeps in. Doubt can deteriorate into guilt or a loss of confidence. Left unattended, doubt can become a downward spiral into the inability to act, crippling our plans, confusing our minds.

Here are how, most successful people I have read about overcome doubts and gotten back on track.

1. **Resolve the unknowns**
If there is one thing that will bring doubts flooding our heart, it is not having enough information about something. The more information you have the less doubtful you will feel.

Doubt is ultimately uncertainty in your decisions or actions; so it makes sense that the more you know about something the more confident you can be in making the right choices. I bet few people would have as many doubts about interviews if they knew what questions were going to be asked and who was asking them!

2. **Have a systematic way to determine when there is doubt**: "Do I have any hesitation to proceed full speed and confidently?" If yes, reconsider before beginning or continuing.

3) **When doubt is obvious, write down your concerns**: Do not just do this as a mental exercise. Keep asking and keep writing until you develop a sense of clarity.

4) **What you can describe, you can conquer**: Once you have written the causes of your doubt, begin to think of solutions. What are the options, alternate courses of action? Do you need to rethink your position? List the answers; develop a proactive approach to implementing them.

5 **Realise that you can manage doubt**: If you wait until you are 100% certain, you will never act. Strive for a balance between the level of uncertainty, the level of risk, and the cost of failure.

6) **Make mid-course corrections frequently**: Reinforce your good decisions. Reduce the impact of your bad ones. Think and act, do not succumb to the "paralysis of analysis."

7) **Get help when you can not figure out a situation by yourself**: There are experts in every field. Find them and use them appropriately.

8) **Push through the doubts** Get to work: Do something. Act in some positive way. We all fail at one time or the other. It is difficult or impossible to succeed without failing. Learn from the failures and continue on an improved course toward success.

When doubt assails you, do what other successful people do. Look at it directly. Determine its causes. Resolve them and get back to enjoying a life of confidence.

DEALING WITH WORRY

We all spend too much time worrying about things that will never materialise and this worry only makes our lives unnecessarily complicated and painful. For most Youth Corpers, the last month of the service year is usually the 'worry month'.

Several hours are normally spent worrying about things that will end in the archives of the mind. Dealing with worry does not only solve immediate problems, it also solves future problems. I present three ways to deal with worry.

1. Take Action

When we worry about things we can become paralyzed by fear. Rather than just worrying, think very carefully about what practical steps you can take to avoid the problem. For example, if you worry about what to do after graduation, you could take a practical step by doing part time jobs. By the time you are doing something, your worry will eventually disappear. I discovered that an idle mind is always a garden for worry.

If you just worry and feel powerless, the problem will not go away, but will continue to lurk in the back of your mind. By taking action and working towards your destination you will feel much better.

Some problems should not be ignored, they require action; however, for other worries there are no steps that you can take because the worry is mostly imaginary. If you realise there is nothing you can actually do, this is a very good reason to stop worrying about it.

2. Be Careful What You Think About
When we think about something intensely we give this idea greater power. In some form these ideas are more likely to materialise.

> When we worry about things we can become paralyzed by fear.

If we worry over making a mistake, we can increase our chances of doing this. We therefore need to be careful what we think about; if we worry over a negative outcome we increase the chance that it will occur – Our worries can become self fulfilling. If we remember the power of thought, we will be more careful about dwelling on painful outcomes. Rather than worrying about a negative event, focus your attention on how difficult situations could be resolved and think how you would successfully deal with the problem.

3. Control Your Thoughts
The key to reducing anxiety and worry is learning the ability to control your thoughts. Sometimes we feel powerless over our own thoughts; it is as if we are slave to them. Whatever thoughts may come we identify with them and accept them as true.

However, this is a big mistake. Our own thoughts are often wrong. Also we do have the ability to decide which thoughts to pursue and which thoughts to reject; if we are determined we can prevent thoughts taking hold and throw them out of our mind. If we give importance to controlling our own mind we will be less subject to pursuing endless worries and anxieties.

There are always things to worry about, but, as it has often been said, worrying is not going to help. Either take practical steps to deal with the problem or do not waste your time worrying about unnecessary things. If you keep ignoring worries, eventually they will go away.

The key is to live in the present moment; when we worry we are thinking of the future or past and this prevents us from enjoying the present moment. To reduce worries and anxieties is not to ignore problems – it means we work toward solutions rather than just thinking of bad outcomes. Worrying does not solve problems; rather it compounds them. Instead of worrying, think solutions; think of various options towards solution of the problem: option A, B,C etc.

Now that we have dealt with the immobilizers, before we proceed let me conclude with this quote

"Fear knocked at the door, Faith answered and nobody was there."

LIFE PRINCIPLES FROM CHAPTER TEN

- *Fear means False Evidence Appearing Real.*
- *Once you know your fears, attack it with prayer.*
- *The more information you have the less doubtful you will feel*
- *When we think about something intensely we give this idea greater power.*
- *When doubt assails you, do what other successful people do. Look at it directly. Determine its causes. Resolve them and get back to enjoying a life of increasing success.*
- *When we worry about things we can become paralyzed by fear.*

CHAPTER 11

"If it is important to you, you will find a way, if not you will find an excuse."

CHAPTER ELEVEN

DEALING WITH LAZINESS AND EXCUSES

"Laziness casts one into a deep sleep, and an idle person will suffer hunger"
-Proverbs 19:15

One of the traps that graduates are likely to fall into is the trap of laziness and apportioning of blames. Playing the blame game actually makes you a lazy person.

The problem with laziness and excuses is that their full effect is not felt for quite a while. It never seems like a little more sleep here and a little more fun there will cause our entire world to crumble. But it is the cumulative effects of our procrastination that can wreak havoc in our lives.

With steady, diligent care you can manage your life well but if you allow yourself to get sidetracked with sleep, idleness or unimportant things, you can quickly lose track of what you need to be doing and become overwhelmed with the irrelevant things of this life.

"I went by the field of the sluggard, by the vineyard of the man void of understanding; Behold, it was all grown over with thorns. Its surface was covered with nettles, and its stone wall was broken down. Then I saw, and considered well. I saw, and received instruction: a little sleep, a little slumber, a little folding of the hands to sleep; so your poverty will come as a robber, and your want as an armed man."
-Proverbs 24:30-34 (WEB)

Continual neglect of what you are supposed to do and the important matters in our lives, even if it does not seem like a big deal at the time, can cause poverty and want to creep up on you – even to the point where you do not realise it until it is too late.

> *If a farmer doesn't plant his seed in the planting season, there will be no harvest in the reaping season.*

In stark contrast, continual care, maintenance, and repair, even though it does not seem much can keep your work running smoothly and help you in dealing with your life much more easily.

Sleep and naps can easily rob you of the time you need to do the very work that will move your life forward. While sleep is necessary and a quick nap may refresh you enough to get some work done, it is easy to fall into the habit of excesses.

Too much sleep and naps can quickly bring you to poverty. You know that you cannot do any work while you are sleeping or napping.

EXCUSE ME, I HAVE AN EXCUSE

Another trap we must avoid is using excuses to avoid doing what you are supposed to do. These excuses can come in all kinds of disguises depending on your circumstances.

I am not saying you should not take out time to rest but we all know how we use excuses and half-truths to get out of some things that we do not feel like doing at a particular time.

If a farmer does not plant his seed in the planting season, there will be no harvest in the reaping season. And if you do not do your work when you need to, there won't be reward.

> *"He who observes the wind will not sow, and he who regards the clouds will not reap*
> - Ecclesiastes 11:7

TAKING UP CHALLENGING TASKS

I define "hard work" as work that is challenging; a work that requires both mental and physical exertion. This kind of work is a key requirement for success.

Some people think of challenging work as painful, stressful or uncomfortable. Does challenging work necessarily have to be painful, stressful or uncomfortable? No, of course not. In fact, a major key to success is to learn to enjoy challenging work and to enjoy working hard at it.

Why take up challenging work? Because challenging work, when intelligently chosen, pays off. It is the work that people of lesser character will avoid. If you avoid challenging work, you avoid doing what it takes to succeed.

To keep your muscles strong or your mind sharp, you need to challenge them. To do only what is easy will lead to physical and mental laziness and very mediocre results, followed by a share waste of time and effort spent justifying why such laziness is okay, instead of stepping up and taking on some real challenges.

TAKE CHARGE OF YOUR LIFE!

There is a common philosophy that says "***go with the flow***"; the negative aspect to this belief system is that you must yield control of your life to that flow. That is okay if you do not mind living passively and letting life happen to you.

If you feel you are here to be tossed about by life's wave instead of to make a formidable impact, then you will have to accept where the flow takes you and learn to like it, but sometimes the flow does not go in the right direction. You can go with the flow and end up in a difficult situation if you do not assume more direct control when needed. Lazy people are more likely to drift along with the flow of life than to do otherwise.

On the other hand, there is the alternative way of looking at life with you as the driving force behind it. You create and control the flow yourself. This is a more challenging way to live but also a much more rewarding one. You are not limited to those experiences that can only be gotten passively or painlessly — now you can have much more of what you want by being willing to accept and take on bigger challenges.

If I only went with the perceived easy flow of my life, I would never have learned how to use the computer; I would not have obtained a University degree. I would not have learnt video editing or media work. Those were all challenges which pitched me against the tide of what was easy and natural but today, I am glad that I went through them.

I certainly would not have written this book if I had yielded (my life) to the flow. One does not exactly flow into such a thing as writing a book, it requires a lot of discipline.

I do believe there is an underlying flow to life at times, but I see myself as a co-creator in that flow. I can ride the flow when it is headed where I want to go, or I can get off and blaze my own trail when necessary.

When you step up and learn to see yourself as the driver of your life instead of the passive victim of it, then it becomes a lot easier to take on big challenges and to endure the hardships they sometimes require. You learn to associate more pleasure to the character development you gain than the minor discomforts you experience.

You should become accustomed to spending more time outside your comfort zone. Many of us spend too much time in our comfort zone. Some even hate being outside their comfort zone. What people with such way of thinking often forget is that nothing worthwhile is achieve in the comfort zone.

> *If you want to achieve some really big and interesting goals, you have to learn to fall in love with hard work.*

Therefore, hard work is something you should embrace because it always leads to tremendous gain and growth. When you embrace hard work, you eventually develop the maturity and responsibility to understand that certain goals will never just flow into your life; they will only happen if you take charge and act as the driving force to bring them to fruition.

WHAT YOU STAND TO LOSE BY AVOIDING HARD WORK

If you refuse to embrace handwork, you will probably never get an education, marry the man or woman of your dream, or even make any significant difference in this world.

You will have to settle for only what going with the flow can provide, which is mediocrity. You will basically just take up space and die without really having mattered.

If you want to achieve some really big and interesting goals, you have to learn to fall in love with hard work. Hard work makes the difference. It is what separates the children from the mature adults.

One of my very close friends once told me that it is so difficulty to be an adult. And I agree completely with him, indeed it is difficult to be an adult, because adults make tough decisions, while children bask in the euphoria of the decisions.

You can keep living as a child and desperately hoping that life will always be easy, but then you will be stuck in a child-like world, working on other people's goals instead of your own; waiting for opportunities to come to you instead of creating your own.

When you learn to embrace hard work instead of running from it, you gain the ability to execute on your big goals, no matter what it takes to achieve them. You blast through obstacles that stop others who have less resolve. But what is it that gets you to that point when you become unstoppable? What gets you to embrace hard work?

PROPELLED BY PURPOSE
"When purpose is not known abuse is inevitable"
-Myles Munrooe

Why do ships sail? Why does an airplane fly? What makes a car move? The ship, airplane and car are all machine. They are often driven by great engines. But what is it that propels their movement?

The ship will remain in the harbor, the airplane will remain on the tarmac in the airport and the car will be parked in the garage without purpose. Purpose is the destination that prompts the journey.

Once there is a man with a destination in the ship, the ship will sail; once there is a man with purpose in the airplane, the airplane will fly the same goes with the car.

If you find out that your life is not heading somewhere, that perhaps you are trapped in the merry-go-round of life, going everywhere but heading nowhere, you probably have not found your purpose yet.

Purpose is the propeller of life without which you are doomed to remain where you have always been. It is only when you have embraced purpose that you are ready to take on life.

When you live for a strong purpose, then hard work is not an option. It is a necessity. If your life has no real purpose, then you can avoid hard work, and it would not matter because you have decided that your life itself does not matter anyway. So who cares if you work hard or take the easy road?

But if you have chosen a significant purpose for your life, it is going to require hard work to get there — any meaningful purpose will require hard work.

You have to admit to yourself then that the only way this purpose is going to be fulfilled is by embracing hard work and this is what takes you beyond fear, doubt and worry. Beyond the lazy crying little child who thinks that hard work is something to run away from.

When you become driven by a purpose greater than yourself, you embrace hard work out of necessity. You assume responsibility for getting jobs done, knowing that without total commitment and a lot of hard work, it is never going to happen.

Show me a person who avoids hard work and I will show you someone who has not found his or her purpose yet because anyone who knows his or her purpose will embrace hard work. That person will pay the price willingly.

If you do not know your purpose yet, then in the world of mature human beings, you do not yet matter. You are just a piece of driftwood on the flow created by those who live with a purpose. If you want to make a difference in the world, then hard work is the price. There are no shortcuts.

Purpose and hard work are two great allies. Purpose is the "why." Hard work is the "how". Purpose is what turns labour into labour of love. It transmutes the pain of hard work into the higher level pleasure of dedication, commitment, resolve and passion. It turns pain into strength, eventually to the point where you do not notice the pain as much as you enjoy the strength.

Let me draw the curtain on this chapter with this quote

> *"If you do not know where you are going, any road will get you there."*
> -Lewis Carroll

LIFE PRINCIPLES FROM CHAPTER ELEVEN

- *Continual neglect of what we are suppose to do and the important matters in our lives, even if it does not seem like a big deal at the time, can cause poverty and want to creep up on us.*
- *If a farmer does not plant his seed in the planting season, there will be no harvest in the reaping season.*
- *If you want to achieve some really big and interesting goals, you have to learn to fall in love with hard work.*
- *Hard work is something you look forward to because you know that it will lead to tremendous growth*
- *Purpose is the propeller of life. Without which you are doomed to remain where you have always been.*

CHAPTER 12

"All that is necessary to break the spell of inertia and frustration is to - act as if it were impossible to fail."
-Dorothea Brande

CHAPTER TWELVE

BREAKING THE FORCE OF INERTIA

"And David was greatly distressed; for the people spake of stoning him, because the soul of all the people was grieved, every man for his sons and for his daughters: but David encouraged himself in the LORD his God."
-1ST Samuel 30:6

Doing ordinary jobs or being an ordinary job service provider requires a lot more than waking up in the morning and smiling to the office because such jobs are undesirable and unattractive. For you to engage yourself in them you must be driven from within, you must be internally motivated.

This is very important because you might not have any external motivation or encouragement from people around you; particularly as a graduate, people will tell you all sort of things. They will discourage you and ask questions like: how can you be doing this kind of job? The key word here is that you must be self-motivated. Above all you must be humble.

There is a force in Physics call *"**the force of inertia**"*. It is one of the strongest forces to overcome before an object can move.

Inertia, according to the Advanced Learner's English Dictionary 7th Edition is defined as *"lack of energy, lack of desire or inability to move."*

W. Clement Stone once said that:

"So many fail because they don't get started - they don't go. They don't overcome inertia. They don't begin."

Breaking the force of inertia is crucial to making progress in life. It requires motivation.

THE ROLLING STONE

"Motivation" is derived from the Latin word *"movere"* which means *to move*. Motivation is the activation or energisation of goal-oriented behaviour (Wikipedia, 2010)[38].

Motivation is the process of arousing, energising, directing and sustaining goal-directed behaviour.

> *Motivation is your internal energy that thrusts your behavior to attain a particular goal.*

Motivation is the inner drive that pushes individuals to act or perform.

From the foregoing we could draw three points about motivation:

- First, motivation is in-built in every human being and only needs to be activated or aroused.
- Second, motivation is temporal as a motivated person at one time can become de-motivated another time. Hence, individual motivation must be sustained and nourished after it has been effectively activated.

---

[38] Wikipedia, 2010 online Encyclopaedia @ www.wikipedia.com

- Third, the essence of individual motivation is to direct the individual's thinking and doing (actions) towards effective and efficient achievement of set goals.

THREE FUNDAMENTAL TRUTHS ABOUT MOTIVATION

i. Motivation is your internal energy that pushes your behaviour to attain a particular goal.
ii. Motivation is your interior power that makes you determined to accomplish a task.
iii. Motivation is the inside force that propels you to do certain job.

Motivation, by definition is an inner drive – and you cannot inject, introduce or infuse this inner willpower into anyone. You cannot force people to be intrinsically motivated.

Nevertheless, if it is true that you cannot motivate people, it is also true that you can create the conditions where others will feel motivated. These are the conditions that most motivational speakers create.

> *Motivation strengthens the ambition, increases initiative and gives direction, courage, energy and the persistence to follow one's goals.*

Motivation is the inner power or energy that pushes toward acting, performing actions and achieving. Motivation has much to do with desire and ambition and if they are absent, motivation is absent too.

Often, a person has the desire and ambition to get something done or achieve a certain goal but lacks the push, the initiative and the willingness to take action. This is due to lack of motivation and inner drive.

Motivation strengthens the ambition, increases initiative and gives direction, courage, energy and the persistence to follow one's goals. A motivated person takes action and does whatever is needed to achieve his/her goals. A motivated person does not wait to be pushed. Most time he is the one that pulls the trigger.

Motivation becomes strong when you have a vision, a clear mental image of what you want to achieve and also a strong desire to actualise it. In this situation, motivation awakens and pushes you forward, toward taking action and making the vision a reality. A motivated person will always find a way to get things done.

Motivation can be applied to every action and situation. There could be motivation to study a foreign language, to get good grades at school, bake a cake, write a poem, write a book, take a walk every day, make more money, get a better job, own a business, or become a writer, a doctor or a lawyer.

Motivation is present whenever there is a clear vision, precise knowledge of what one wants to do, a strong desire and faith in one's abilities.

Motivation is one of the most important keys to success. When there is lack of motivation you either get no results, or only mediocre results, whereas when there is motivation you attain greater and better results and achievements.

Compare a student who lacks motivation and who hardly studies to a student who is highly motivated and who devotes many hours to his studies; they will get absolutely different grades.

> *A motivated person is a happier person, more energetic, and sees the positive end result in his/her mind.*

Lack of motivation shows lack of enthusiasm, zest and ambition, whereas the possession of motivation is a sign of strong desire, energy and enthusiasm and the willingness to do whatever it takes to achieve what one sets out to do. A motivated person is a happier person, more energetic, and sees the positive end result in his/her mind.

TEN WAYS TO KEEP YOUR MOTIVATION HIGH

What can you do to enhance your motivation and awaken the power that will push you toward accomplishing your dreams, small and big?

Here are a few suggestions:

i. **Set a goal**: If you have a major goal, it would be a good idea if you split it into several minor goals, each small goal leading to your major goal. In this way, you will find it easier to motivate yourself, as you will not feel overwhelmed by the size of your goal and the things you have to do, and the goal would seem more feasible and easier to accomplish.

ii. **Be a finisher**: Understand that finishing what you start is important. Hammer into your mind that whatever you start you have to finish. Develop the habit of going to the finish line.

iii. **Interact with achievers:** Socialise with achievers and people with similar interests or goals since motivation

iv. **Do not procrastinate:** Never procrastinates. Procrastination leads to laziness and laziness leads to lack of motivation.

v. **Persist until you succeed:** Persistence, patience and not giving up despite failure and difficulties keep up the motivation to succeed.

vi. **Read books**: Read about the subjects of your interest. This will keep your enthusiasm and ambition alive.

vii. **Speak to yourself:** Constantly affirm to yourself that you can and will succeed.

viii. **Create a photo book**: Look at photos of things you want to get, achieve or do.

ix. **See it in with your minds eyes:** Visualise your goals with happiness and joy.

x. **Pray constantly.** What you pray constantly about will likely become your passion. Your passion is the oil of your motivation.

Remember, if a certain goal is really important, you need motivation to keep you going.

RELEASING YOUR TEN INNER POWERS

We all possess various inner powers but they are often in a dormant state. Sometimes, due to various unpredictable circumstances, some of these powers might manifest unexpectedly and temporarily. **What are these inner powers?**

i. **The Power Of Concentration**
   "...But Jesus stooped down, and with his finger wrote on the ground, as though he heard them not. So when they continued asking him, he lifted up

> *himself, and said unto them, He that is without sin among you, let him first cast a stone at her. And again he stooped down, and wrote on the ground."*
> -John 8:6-7

This is the ability of focusing the attention on one single object or thought and at the same time excluding all other unrelated thoughts from the mind.

Concentrating on one single thought or subject directs the mental energies to one point and prevents their dissipation. Concentration strengthens the power of the thought focused on and can achieve wonders. This action is similar to the action of a magnifying glass that concentrates the rays of the sun into one single beam, and which can then burn a piece of paper.

ii.   Decisiveness

This is the inner strength to make decisions, take action and handle and execute any task, regardless of inner resistance, discomfort or difficulty. It manifests as inner firmness, decisiveness, determination, resolution and persistence.

iii.   Self-discipline

This inner power manifests as the ability to forgo instant gratification in favor of something better and of the giving up of instant pleasure and satisfaction for a higher goal. It is the ability of an individual to stick to actions, thoughts and behaviour and which leads to improvement and success.

iv.   The power of imagination

This is the ability to experience a whole world inside the mind. Imagination is a creative power. Imagination is the formation of images of your desired destination in your mind. By training and using it correctly one can create and attract health, wealth, happiness and favourable events and circumstances.

Imagination is not limited only to seeing pictures in the mind. Feelings and sensations relating to all the five senses can be imagined too. It is possible to imagine sounds, tastes, scents, physical sensations, feelings and emotions.

A well developed and strong imagination does not make one a daydreamer or an unrealistic person. On the contrary, it strengthens the creative abilities, the ability to solve problems and is a great tool for recreating and remodeling one's life and circumstances.

When you know how to work with it you can make our heart" desires come true.

v.   Persistence
It is so easy to stop and give up when one's plans do not turn out as expected or take too much time to accomplish. Persistence manifests as the inner strength to continue in spite of difficulties, obstacles and failure.

vi.   Motivation
Motivation is an inner driving force which directs one toward a chosen aim or goal. In order to accomplish anything, one needs a driving, directing power, otherwise nothing would happen, and motivation supplies this power.

vii.   Vision - Guided –Ambition (VGA)
When your ambition is guided by a vision, you are likely to get to your destination with precision. Wishful thinking is not strong enough to make one take action. A wish is a weak desire. Only a strong desire can drive one forward, to take action, follow plans and accomplish desires and goals.

viii.   Self-confidence
this is faith in one's abilities, strength and power. Confidence leads to courage, doing things, trying new things and to success.

ix.   Detachment
This is the ability to remain calm and uninvolved on the emotional and mental levels. This ability saves one a lot of trouble, discomfort, fears and worries. Detachment helps one to accept calmly what cannot be changed and go on with one's life. Detachment leads to inner balance and peace.

x.   Peace of Mind
A peaceful mind is free from the compulsion of incessant and restless thinking and worrying. When thoughts do not disturb the tranquility of the mind one experiences inner happiness. A person possessing peace of mind is calm and in control of himself. Such a person retains inner balance under almost all conditions and is hardly affected by negative circumstances and situations.

To bring this chapter to a close, let us consider a beautiful car without a spark plug. No matter how hard you may try, the car cannot move. In the same way no matter how big our dreams are, without motivation, our dreams might just end up as dreams.

LIFE PRINCIPLES FROM CHAPTER TWELVE

- *Motivation is your internal energy that thrusts your behavior to attain a particular goal.*
- *A motivated person will always find a way to get things done.*
- *A motivated person is a happier person, more energetic, and sees the positive end result in his/her mind.*
- *Motivation strengthens the ambition, increases initiative and gives direction, courage, energy and the persistence to follow one's goals.*

Wake up! Take This Job!

CHAPTER

13

"Opportunity is missed by most people because it is dressed in overalls and looks like work."

– Thomas Edison

CHAPTER THIRTEEN

THE JOB SHIFT

"Do not be afraid to give your best to what seemingly are small jobs. Every time you conquer one it makes you that much stronger. If you do the little jobs well, the big ones will tend to take care of themselves."
-Dale Carnegie

In September 2000, at Millennium Summit - the largest-ever gathering of Heads of State and Government - resolved to "**develop and implement strategies that give young people everywhere a real chance to find decent and productive work**.[39]"

This commitment forms part of a global partnership for development, to be implemented by governments, employers' and workers' representatives, civil society and young people.

This resolution is called the Millennium Development Goal (MDG). The Secretary General of the United Nations, in his report to the Millennium Assembly, highlighted the need to **"explore imaginative approaches to this difficult challenge."**

Access to decent and productive work that provides an adequate income is the surest way of increasing your

---
[39] http://www.un.org/ga/search/view_doc.asp?symbol=A/55/PV.8&Lang=E

Wake up! Take This Job!

contribution to the future prosperity of this country and your immediate community.

But to secure a decent job in an environment like ours with its attendant economic instability is a very hard nut to crack.

It has been said that ***"to do the same thing over and over again and to expect a different result is the definition of insanity"***. For you to get a job in a jobless economy you must change your strategy, you must do things differently.

In this chapter I have proposed an approach that will help solve the problem of joblessness. Although this approach is not novel, it has not been judiciously taken advantage of by most people; the approach has been used all over the world and has worked immensely.

This approach is the very foundation of Small and Medium Scale Enterprise and Industries (SMEIs). It is the foundation upon which most multinational companies are built. I believe in it very strongly because I have practiced it and it worked.

Let me shed more light on the United Nation's Declaration at the beginning of the millennium with regards to **'*young people having decent and productive work*'.**

What constitute a decent job? In Warri, for instance many young people express a strong preference for offshore oil and gas jobs; their preference is not because the jobs are but that the salary is attractive.

Wake up! Take This Job!

But to be realistic, some of the jobs that Niger Delta youths do offshore are not really decent jobs. They do it because of the money.

From the foregoing, we could reasonably infer that a job is only as decent as the amount of money it generates or the exposure and experience it gives to the person who does the job.

It therefore means that a decent job is not determined by the dress code but how much the doer of such job receives as his take-home pay when the job is done and the satisfaction he or she derives from the job.

> *A job is only as decent as the amount of money it produces and the exposure and experience it gives to the person that does the job.*

WHAT MANNER OF JOB IS THIS?

There are two basic types of jobs in this world. These jobs have been classified by dress code

1. **White colla**r: The conventional corporate jobs and
2. **Blue collar:** The unconventional ordinary jobs.

1.   THE CONVENTIONAL CORPORATE JOBS.

More often than not, when a Nigerian graduate steps out of school, his or her eyes are fixed on the conventional uncommon, high wage job. Jobs of this category are corporate, high-profile and are tagged white collar jobs.

Examples are private sector jobs like banking, insurance, oil and gas, and public sector jobs (Federal, State and Local Government jobs in the civil service). Professional jobs like law, medical related disciplines and Engineering also falls into this category.

Most graduates who complain about not having a job are actually referring to this category of jobs. It is presumed that jobs of this categorisation are highly secured with better pay and it commands respect from people.

2. THE UNCONVENTIONAL ORDINARY JOBS

There is however a second category-the uncelebrated, unconventional ordinary jobs. This is the path not frequently taken by Nigerian graduates; but sometime on the road less travelled, there could be a treasure chest hidden somewhere.

While the struggle continues to get the high profile jobs, there are considerably large employment opportunities in the informal sector which an individual can take advantage of.

People however presume that the unconventional, ordinary jobs in the informal sector are low wage jobs and because of this mindset, most graduates simply avoid engaging in such jobs.

LEAPING LEPERS

By definition, lepers are a group of people that are ostracised and excluded from the normal people because of their disease. Leprosy causes changes in the body which are often evident in a person's appearance.

Persons with leprosy cannot hide their disease. It is visible on their faces and bodies. They are often camped outside the city in place called Leprosarium

They have all the biological features of a human being; they have a normal brain, they can be educated, they can have children but they are lepers, and as such are excluded from the community. They are not welcome to live with normal people.

A graduate without a job might fit the description of a leper. The story of Naaman in the Bible depicts the life of a typical Nigerian graduate.

> *'The king of Aram had high admiration for Naaman, the commander of his Army, because through him the Lord had given Aram victories. But though Naaman was a mighty warrior, he suffered from leprosy"*
> -2 kings 5:1

Let us put it in a way that fits a graduate: "he had a first class or a second class honour; he is a very brilliant person, with great prospect. But he is jobless."

My Pastor, Reverend Bill Awaritoma once preached a sermon from this story titled **"kicking the "but" out of your life"**. You must kick the "but" of joblessness out of your life. How do you do that? Let us look at the story of the four lepers in the Holy writ.

> *"Now there were four men with leprosy sitting at the entrance of the city gates. "Why should we sit here waiting to die?" they asked each other. We will starve if we stay here, and we will starve if we go back into the city. If we go out and surrender to the Aramean army. If they let us live, so much better, but if they kill us we would have died any way."*
> -2 king 7: 3-4(NIV)

The four lepers had come to a point in their lives when they must decide what path to take. Their options were clear; they could remain at the gate (like a graduate waiting at the gate of the employers of labour for the white collar job) and starve to death or face the risk of moving out.

Wake up! Take This Job!

They decided to take the path not frequently travelled. They decided to kick the "but" out of their lives by moving out.

In the path less travelled, there could be thorns, there could be reptiles, branches of trees that have grown out of proportion may form barriers on the way; there could be serious danger. All these make the path undesirable, such that nobody wants to go through it. It is like the valley of the shadow of death but With all its attendant risk, the four lepers were undeterred, unafraid and willing to try; they stepped out boldly into the path and ended up with joy and gladness.

> *If you wait at the gate of the employers of labour for the white collar jobs, you might remain stuck with the "but" of joblessness for a long time.*

This story is a typical reflection of most Nigerian youth. If you wait at the gate of the employers of labour for the white collar jobs, you might remain stuck with the "but" of joblessness for a long time and you might even die waiting.

THE TURTLE'S ADVENTURE

You have to stick your neck out. You have to take a risk, like the turtle. In order for a turtle to move it must stick its neck out. When a turtle sticks its neck (and head) out, it becomes more vulnerable (in the open) to predators. But a turtle must leave the safe haven of its shell to eat and make progress. This reminds me of a similar phrase I have heard: "**Behold the turtle. He only makes progress when he sticks his neck out.**"
Just like the turtle, you have to stick your neck out, you may need to take your journey through the path least

travelled, however, in that path you might find something that is really pleasant.

If you enter into the arena of unconventional jobs, you never can tell what you will find. You might discover something that may not only put money in your pocket, but might even save the entire country.

The lepers leaped from emptiness, destitution and hunger to abundance, plenty and satisfaction. Their discovery not only put food on their table but saved the entire nation of Israel.

All these happened because they dared to step out. I challenge you to step out from wherever you have been hibernating and put your foot in the murky waters of common jobs. You will get dirty, you might be scorned, but at the end you will smile.

You can take that leap of faith today.

FINDING THE ORDINARY JOBS

Ordinary jobs are everywhere. That is why they are common. Most common jobs are part time jobs. Finding part-time jobs, might pave the way for you to get a fulltime job.

Look at the "ordinary jobs", they are not desirable, they are not attractive and they are not appealing but they are things that must be done. They are everywhere but only few people are taking advantage of them. They are in the neighbourhood, in the church, in the schools, everywhere you go, you will definitely find them. Common jobs are like gold fish they cannot hide.

If you have focused on the conventional, high profile corporate jobs in the public or private sector and you are yet to find one, why not shift your focus to the unconventional jobs in the informal sector.

WHERE ARE THE UNCOMMON JOBS?

i. **The Church**: people often neglect this great platform of employment; there are numerous jobs within the church. If you are committed in the church you already have an advantage, people are likely to trust you. All you need to do is to let them know that you can do a certain job. For example, laundry and dry cleaning. You could be the sole dry cleaner in your church and you will be smiling to the bank every week.

If you can play any musical instrument, then you have no business with unemployment. The church is in the lookout for people like you. *"Your gift will make room for you and bring you before great people"*.

The church is an organised market for any product that brings glory and honour to Christ. If you target your local congregation in the development of your products and services, I am sure you will break even within a short time.

ii. **Schools:** Private schools are springing up everywhere, some are in their fledging stage and your services might be needed. They might need the service of individuals to typeset their examinations question papers. All you need to do is to walk up to the school, talk to the owner or the administrator. Let them know the kind of services you render.

If you try one, two or three schools, I am sure that at least one will consider you.

With the recent introduction of online registration with biometrics for examination, another avenue for employment has opened up for you; you could do online registration for examinations such as WAEC, NECO and JAMB for schools and private candidate. If you can get about five schools, I am sure by the time the job is done you will be smiling to the bank.

iii. **Higher institutions:** The unconventional jobs in the higher institutions are enormous; in fact they are so many that, you could just stay back in your school after graduation and start earning a living.

- **Research assistance:** by the time a student gets to final year, he needs a lot of assistance in carrying out his or her research; you could step in here and provide the necessary assistance at a price.
- **Project typing/binding:** every final year student must typeset his or her project. You could take the contract of typing for a whole class. But be sure, you have reliable hands that could do the typesetting for you.
- Other business opportunities abound in the school or around the school. Look closely and you will find them.

iv. **Neighbourhood:** Your neigbhourhood is a gold mine. Every neighbourhood has a gold mine. Take a walk around where you live, you will see opportunities. Some of the opportunities could include, home teaching, laundry and dry cleaning services, clearing of the environment including refuse disposal.

v. **Building Sites:** You do not need to be a brick layer or an iron bender to visit a building site or an area that is fast developing. Most builders engage the services of individuals such as painters, electricians, labourers, cement suppliers etc. You can arrange with the owner of the building or the builder to bring these people that will do the finishing for the project at a price. All you need is the courage to say that you can do it.

vi.   **The Agricultural sector:** Nobody can live without food. There are enormous job opportunities in the agricultural and agro-allied sectors graduate. This range from fishing farming to transportation of agro-allied products. It pays to do food business.

vii. Finally, I can not give an exhaustive list of all the avenues of ordinary jobs in this book, what I want you to know is that they are everywhere. Just be on the lookout and you will surely find them.

ORDINARY JOB SERVICES PROVIDERS

Although technology keeps advancing, where a task that takes an hour in the past, can now be completed within minutes. 'Time' still remains the most precious amenity in life.

As people become busier by the day, some of them find it harder to carry out some of their daily chores that take up a good part of their precious time. Most people simply do not have time for these daily chores and resort to hiring others to run these everyday jobs for them.

This situation has opened up an important aspect of the ordinary job industry that I call: **Ordinary Job Service Providers (OJSP)**.

An ordinary job service provider does not necessary do the ordinary jobs by himself. He gets other people to do the ordinary jobs for him.

He is the link between the owner of the job and the doer of the jobs. This aspect of ordinary job gives one time to concentrate on other important things. What it means is that, you could be a general contractor, you could take the job as a contract and get someone else (a sub contractor) to do it for you.

For instance, there was a time I went round private schools and gathered their examinations questions, took them to a business centre and asked them to do the computer typesetting and photocopying. After which I paid them for the services rendered and took the completed work back to the schools, I was handsomely paid for the services.

You could take up a painting job; you do not necessary need to know how to paint. There are painters everywhere. Once you get the painting job give it to a painter as a contract. You could take up a clearing job for a project site and get people to do the clearing.

There are countless ways to generate income as an ordinary job service provider. All you need to do is to be on the lookout for opportunities.

SEVEN FUNDAMENTAL REASONS WHY MOST PEOPLE AVOID THE ORDINARY JOBS

i.   **Pride**

Pride is a killer of destiny. Most people avoid the so called common jobs because of pride. They see themselves bigger than such jobs but the truth is that such people are small inside. People with such attitude seldom make progress in life. It is true that it is not all jobs that you can do, there are certain jobs that you can do that will not diminish you one bit but because of pride, you may deny yourself of the benefit of doing such job.

ii. **What People Will Say**

Wake up! Take This Job!

"So what do you do for a living?" is a common enough question when engaging in small talk with somebody you have just met. An answer to this question tends to expose almost everything about you that you wish to hide, particularly if you are not doing the so-called big job. This single question is one reason why many people shy away from ordinary jobs.

There is a category of people that we call "men pleasers', they always want to be applauded for every decision they make. Perhaps, you fall into this category; I want you to know that as long as you are out to please the crowd you may not get to the cloud.

If you do not blow your trumpet, nobody will blow it for you. If you are doing the so called ordinary jobs, be proud of it. If you display an attitude of pride in what you do, before long people will begin to respect you for it.

I know a young graduate who started a refuse disposal job single-handedly. He started with an ordinary truck used by truck pushers. Today, he has three Toyota trucks, a car, a well-furnished office and people working for him. He is now a managing director of his own company.

You have to come to terms with the fact that if you are not doing anything to earn a living, people will talk; if you are doing ordinary jobs people will talk; if you are even doing the big jobs people will still talk.

So it is better to do what your conscience tells you and forget about the opinion of the crowd. As long as you are out to please the crowd, you may not get the crown. Do not be men pleasers, do your thing!

> *"If you do not seriously offend at least one person a day, you are not saying or doing enough"*
> — Dan Kennedy

The opinion of the crowd is not constant; when you please them they will sing your praise, when you fail to please them they will shout "crucify him". So, what will you do about the opinion of others? I give you a two word answer: **ignore it**.

Forget their opinion because in the long run it does not count.

iii. The Pay Is Small And Irregular

The scripture admonished us not to despise the days of small beginnings. Drops of water make a mighty ocean. If you refuse to do the common, how will you be able to manage the uncommon? If the pay is irregular and you cannot manage it, do you think that it will be easier to manage when it becomes regular? Pause and think about it. People that cannot manage small pay can hardly manage big pay.

iv. It Is Below My Qualification

Many graduates avoid doing ordinary jobs because they believe that it is below their qualification. True to it, there many jobs that a graduates cannot do. For instance, nobody expect you to be a gate keeper as a graduate.

The truth is that there are jobs that you can do that are below your qualification. Actually, taking a job that is below your qualification, could pave the way for you to get the one that is even above your qualification.

v. Ignorance

What you do not know can kill you. Ignorance can imprison you and rob you of your chances of succeeding in life. Ignorance is darkness. You may not be able to see the potentials that are in the common jobs and as such you might just handle it with levity and feel that it will not take you anywhere

vi.　Lack Of Vision And Foresight
Everything we do is tied to the vision that we have. If you have a great vision, you should know that nothing great starts great, everything big started small. What you call a common job today might become the most sought after job tomorrow.

vii.　Lack Of Adaptability Skill
Some people do not have that basic human skill of survival called adaptability. If things are not the way they want it to be they are grounded; they can not make a detour; they are stuck and will remain where they are.

For you to make significant progress in life you must be adaptive. You must be flexible. Many graduates cannot adapt to the changes that are happening in the society and as a consequence are merely watching their life pass them by. People with such mindset can hardly succeed in this world.

Take a good look at the above seven reasons, are they really strong enough to hold you back? If you think they are not, then remove your eyes from them and get ready to put your knowledge to work.

According Senator Robert Kennedy *"it is from numberless diverse acts of courage and belief that human history is shaped. Each time a man stands up for an ideal or acts to improve the lot of others, or strikes out injustice, he sends forth a tiny ripple of hope."*

Your action today may be a source of hope for someone else tomorrow.

LIFE PRINCIPLES FROM CHAPTER THIRTEEN

- *To do the same thing over and over again and to expect a different result is the definition of insanity.*
- *A job is only as decent as the amount of money it produces and the exposure and experience it gives to the person that does the job.*
- *A graduate without a job might fit the description of a leprous person.*
- *If you wait at the gate of the employers of labour for the white collar jobs, you might remain stuck with the "but" of joblessness*

CHAPTER 14

"I had to make my own living and my own opportunity! But I made it! Don't sit down and wait for the opportunities to come. Get up and make them!"

- Madam C.J. Walker,
Creator of a popular line of African-American hair care products and America's first black female millionaire

CHAPTER FOURTEEN

ORDINARY JOBS WITH EXTRAORDINARY POTENTIALS

"If you will not work until you get your dream job, you are lazy and operating outside of faith. But if you excel in little jobs, they will pave way for the dream job to come."
-Pastor E.A. Adeboye

To help you with identifying ordinary jobs, I have listed and explained twenty five jobs that are presumed to be ordinary. I have taken time to research the jobs that are listed and explained below and I have concluded that, if you could really try your hands on any of them that might interest you, it will be very, very beneficial to you financially.

If you read through carefully, you will definitely see something that interests you. Engaging in any of the under listed job does not require extra intelligence, it does not need any special skill.

You do not need an office, a computer or even a registered company for a start, you may not need tax clearance, government permission or any of those things that big corporate firm need before you start. All that is required is your willingness to try.

"There is not a moment without something to do."
- Cicero

Wake up! Take This Job!

25 ORDINARY JOBS/BUSINESSES WITH EXTRAORDINARY POTENTIALS.

Some of these jobs are dirty, some are boring and some just plain weird, but they all have one thing in common. People cannot live without them; they also have extraordinary potentials for financial returns if you apply yourself diligently to them. Remember, you do not necessary have to do it yourself. You could hire someone to do it for you. If you are humble you can do some of them yourself.

1. ELECTRICAL WORKS/CONTRACTOR

If you read electrical engineering or a related discipline or perhaps you had training in electrical matters, this section is for you.

What it entails

An individual who takes up electrical works installs wiring, fuses and other electrical components in homes, new houses, business premises and factories.

He or she also maintains the wiring. In addition to working with high voltage wiring; those involve in this job also install and maintain voice, data and video wiring. They can either specialize in maintenance or installation, but many work in both areas.

Requirements

A B.Eng, OND, Bsc graduate in Engineering is qualified for this job. If you are not in the line of engineering and you wish to engage in electrical repairs you must be trained and also combine your training instruction with on-the-job training under the supervision of an experienced electrician or Electrical Engineer.

2. AUTOMOBILE REPAIRS

If you have an obsession with cars or passionate about solving mechanical problems, consider a career as an auto repair technician.

Auto repair technicians diagnose car problems and facilitate the necessary repairs using their thorough knowledge of vehicle components and automotive technology.

In today's fast-paced world, people cannot usually do without their cars for a long time. That is why the automobile repairer is in high demand.

It is a good time to become an auto repair technician, particularly in this economic environment when people are holding on to their older cars because they can not afford new ones and even those who could afford new ones need an expert to help maintain them.

Opportunities in Automobile Repair

There are marked opportunities in doing this job. For instance, some companies that utilize official cars and government agencies may retain an auto technician as a part time staff to maintain cars and other vehicles. Majority of auto repair technicians are self-employed contractors, who choose when, where and on what type of cars to work.

3. SOUND ENGINEER

A sound engineer is a technical media professional who operates recording and amplification machines and equipment. He is used in a variety of settings including recording studios, theatres, concert venues, convention centres and churches

Wake up! Take This Job!

Sound engineers/technicians are required to assemble, operate and maintain the technical equipment used to record, amplify, enhance, mix or reproduce sound.

They identify the sound requirements for a given task or situation and perform the appropriate actions to produce this sound. Sound engineers/technicians of different types are required in a range of industries including film, broadcasting (radio or television), live performance (theatre, music, dance, worship service and other religious gathering, election campaign), advertising and audio recordings.

Experience and Training: You must have firsthand experience and training in all the aspects of sound listed below.

- Sound effects,
- Music and Foley editing,
- Recording techniques ,
- Sound equipment operation,
- Amplification,
- Synchronization and Recording software

The service of a sound engineer is in high demand in churches today. Whether the church is big or small, there is no substitute for good sound output.

When sound is produced within the four walls of the church, it is different from when it is produced in other places. Sounds produced in the church must glorify God. Therefore, as a sound engineer in the church you must take cognizance that what you do is very important to what the pastor does.

4.   **COMPUTER SALES /MARKETERS**

Wake up! Take This Job!

This is not to be confused with a computer technician or engineer. A computer salesperson (often called an IT sale professional) delves into the business of selling computer hardware and software. An IT sales professional's job is also to offer support for the hardware and software that is sold and to serve as a liaison between computer hardware companies/distributors and consumers.

What it entails.
The main function of an IT sales professional is to serve as a link between the customer and the supplier, and effectively meet the needs of both parties. The sales professional must recognise the needs of the consumer and provide detailed information to the consumer about the technical specifications of the computer hardware/software offered. The sales professional is responsible for negotiating a price for the sale that is beneficial to the consumer and the supplier, and providing adequate technical support for the merchandise after it is purchased.

Training and Education
Training for an IT sales professional varies, but a simple requirement is on-the-job training. A graduate degree in marketing, business/management, business information systems and mathematics is okay, as the skills acquired throughout these degree programmes can be directly applied to a sales in IT.

5. **COMPUTER SERVICES PROVIDER/ENGINEER**
These include such services as computer assembly and repair, software installation and general maintenance.
Experience
Computer service provider must have had previous computer training in hardware repairs and installation. A computer analyst/ engineer must be good in computer

networking, data base management and assembly of computer accessories.

Qualification:
You do not necessarily need to be a graduate of Computer Science or Computer Engineering, but should have sound ICT knowledge and basic technical know-how on computer hardware repairs and software installation.

6. COMPUTER TUTORS
A computer tutor should be able to teach the basics of computer which is called Computer Appreciation. The package includes Microsoft Office Programmes such as MS-word, PowerPoint, Excel spreadsheet and the use of the internet, browsing, Facebooking, how to upload documents, pictures and videos to the internet.

Experience
You must have had training in Microsoft office packages, CorelDraw, Photoshop and other computer programmes. You must be very patient, tolerant and have the ability to impart knowledge.

7. GRAPHIC DESIGNER
Graphic design is all around us. If you take a moment to notice design in the objects around you, you will see that someone put a thought into making them both functional and appealing. Look at a book or magazine, go to a shop, or take a drive around town. When you do, you will encounter graphic designs. From websites, company logos, road signs, digital banners to product packaging.

Design is an integral part of modern life.

The service of a graphic designer is indispensible. It is in high demand by printers and publishers in particular.

Responsibility
A graphic designer use computer software to generate new images. Draw and print charts, graphs, illustrations, and other artwork, using computer. He or she design posters, greeting cards and wedding cards. Must be conversant with printing, both digital and computer colour separation.

A graphic designer should be creative, with an eye for detail. He or she does not necessarily need to be an OND, HND OR BSC holder in Computer Science or Computer Engineering. However, he or she must have sound ICT knowledge.

8. EVENT PLANNING AND DECORATIONS
Event planning is one of the few careers which mix work and fun. Event planning can be the most exciting jobs but it also requires a lot of skills and hard work.

The career of an event planner offers fun, excitement and job satisfaction but like any other career, there is a lot of hard work involved in event planning. It is a job which requires you to handle multiple responsibilities at any given time. As a planner is expected to make every event a grand success, there is a lot of stress involved too.

Job Description
Event planners are people who go about arranging, coordinating and organizing things for planning a particular event, as may be required by their clients. The planners work hard to organize the event from the planning stage to the actual day of the event. The professional event planners should have a wide expertise in managing all designated tasks without any hiccups.

Corporate Planners

Corporate planners are the professionals, who plan, arrange and organise every aspect of corporate meetings and events. They need to have good communication skills; they need to understand the exact requirements and needs of their clients. Sometimes, they also suggest or choose the best-suited venue for the event which will have all the amenities that the client needs.

Wedding Planners

The demand for the wedding planner is increasing day by day. The main thing that is required of a wedding planner is innovative and creative ideas to organise the event in such a way that the people remember the event for a long time. Apart from arranging all the amenities at the wedding venue, he has to take care of the decoration of the venue, arrange for food and refreshments by contacting the suppliers. Sometimes they are also required to suggest some attractive outfits for marriage.

Outdoor decoration: This is a subset of event planning. An outdoor decorator works with fabrics, flowers and other accessories to make the place or venue of an event a combination of beauty and class. An outdoor decorator must be very creative, as each location may require different decorations and design.

9. INTERIOR DECORATORS

Interior decorators create functional, yet beautiful, spaces. They decorate homes, shops, offices and other professional environments. Interior decorators work directly with clients, giving them advice on which colour schemes, layouts, wallpaper and furniture would be best for a particular space. Interior decorators are responsible for choosing paint colours, lighting, window coverings, furniture and flooring as well as artwork, pillows, rugs and other accessories. They also organise and supervise the arrangement and installation of furnishings.

Experience and training:
Interior decorators should have a good sense of style, creativity, awareness of the latest fashion trends and the determination to succeed in their field.

10.   VIDEOGRAPHY
Videographers, also known as cameramen or camera operators, are responsible for capturing images and recordings on video tape. Often it is the responsibility of a videographer to bring imagination and artistry to their videos. Videographers shoot many different types of video: church messages, news and sports, documentaries, films, television programmes and music videos. Videographers might travel a great deal (to record events like marriages, burials, political programmes)

Experience and training
Some videographers begin their training with formal education, either individual course in camera operation or degrees in video production. Many however work as assistants, setting up cameras, lights, and other equipment, before getting behind the camera.

Qualification
There are no set academic qualifications for entry into this career.

11.   PHOTOGRAPHY
Professional photographers' work can appear anywhere from newspapers and magazines to wedding albums and textbooks.

Wake up! Take This Job!

Professional photography covers a wide range of different specialisation. Each job - or shoot - will be different, and how individual photographers spend their time will depend on the area in which they work. Most photographers work unsociable and irregular hours, including evenings and weekends. Freelance photographers need to be flexible about when they work.

Photographers can work anywhere, from peoples' homes to war zones, laboratories to a music concert. Photography is a very competitive occupation

Experience and training:
Many photographers start work and then get trained on the job. A photographer should be creative, with a good eye for a picture, be reliable and able to meet deadlines; he or she should be motivated and determined; should have excellent technical and photographic skills.

In addition having computer skills, especially with computer programmes such as Photoshop is an added advantage.

He or she should have good communications skills, be confident organising people, be able to listen and interpret the client's needs and be able to focus on getting a good picture no matter what is going on around him.

He or she should have commercial awareness and be good at marketing himself. Some specialist areas of photography have formal training schemes but on the whole there is no set training pattern.

12. GARDENING/LANDSCAPING
The world is going green. Everyone wants to be environmental friendly; homes are being reconstructed to look 'green'. Cities are developing parks, recreations

Wake up! Take This Job!

gardens, and tourists centre are being developed. Golf courses are emerging in new area, old ones need maintenance. Who will take care of them? Your guess is as good as mine. A gardener/ landscaper of course. I mean a professional landscaper. You could be the one.

What it entails
A landscaper or an horticulturist plans and executes small scale landscaping operations and maintains grounds and landscape of private and business residences: Participates with labourer's in preparing and grading terrain, applying fertilizers, seeding and sodding lawns, and transplanting shrubs and plants, using manual and power-operated equipment.

13.　VIDEO EDITING/MULTIMEDIA
A film or video editor is responsible for assembling raw video material into a finished product suitable for broadcasting. The material they work with may consist of raw camera footage, dialogue, sound effects, graphics and special effects.

Majority of film/video editors are employed on a freelance basis, working on short-term or part-time contracts for post-production studios, television companies, churches. Editors may work on a variety of productions including feature films, television programmes, music videos, church messages/sermons, corporate training videos or advertisements.

Video editing is not a difficult to learn. The basic requirement is computer knowledge, a good trainer and the patients to wait for the video you have worked on to be produced.

14.　BOOK EDITOR

Wake up! Take This Job!

Book editors do largely what you would assume. They Plan, coordinate, or edit content of material for publication.

One of the most important things book editors do is acquire books. If you love books and love to read, a job as an editor can be a dream comes true.

Another aspect of an editor's job entails cultivating relationships with authors. Writers, who have good relationships with their editors,will often follow the editors as they change jobs over the years. This means that editors who work with high-profile writers are often more valuable to publishers, since they usually bring big clients with them.

Book Doctors
Book doctors-who also call themselves book editors--are independent contractors who, for a fee, will help an author polish his/her manuscript before submission for publication. As with any profession, there are those who take advantage of their clients' ignorance or confidence, and anyone seeking to hire an editor to help "fix" a book should always exercise caution.

Education Requirements for a Book Editor
A bachelor's degree or a higher degree is required for work as a book editor. Degrees in English, Law, Journalism or Communications are an advantage; however, degrees in other fields can also lead to work as a book editor if the individual has the necessary knowledge and experience.

Editors should have a particular interest in the technical aspects of writing, such as grammar, punctuation and sentence structure. They must also have the ability to work closely with authors and guide them through the publishing process. Editors should possess excellent written and verbal communication skills, a strong academic record and a keen interest in book publishing.

15. E-SERVICES

Just as the world is going e-crazy; so also is Nigeria catching up with the trend. E-services provision is still an emerging business opportunity that has not fully been tapped.

E-business provides opportunities for your business to use digital media to generate revenue for yourself. E-business (doing business on the Internet) can enable small scale businesses in emerging markets gain greater bargaining power in the global economic exchange despite their limited capital and mobility. The world economy is moving online.

Under the umbrella of providing e-services; you can find the following fast growing business opportunities: E-payment, bulk SMS services, Web design and hosting, database management services, e-portal management, online registration for examination etc.

Online Registration

Presently, almost all jobs and examinations in Nigeria today require online application and registration. This is an avenue for you to make good money.

16.   WRITING AND PUBLISHING BOOKS

According to Encyclopedia Britannica, an author is *"one who is the source of some form of intellectual or creative work; especially one who composes a book, article, poem, play or other literary work intended for publication."*

Authors create original work. Writers and authors develop original written materials for books, magazines, trade journals, online publications, company newsletters, radio and television broadcasts, motion pictures and advertisements.

Skills
For this career, you will obviously need strong writing skills and a sense of creativity as well as the interpersonal skills necessary for working with editors, clients, publishers and other related professionals. You should have the following skills if you want to succeed as a writer:

- Ability to organize your thoughts and write them down.
- Ability to read and draw conclusions from written works.
- Ability to write and stitch written materials together.
- Computer proficiency will be an added advantage.
- Drive and the determination to start and finish your write-up are two indispensable attribute for a writer and
- Ability to work in solitude

17. PLAYING OF MUSICAL INSTRUMENTS

Gone are the days when musical instruments were played in churches and at public functions for free. In this present dispensation of monetization of talents and ideas everything is paid for.

Responsibility
Playing musical instruments such as drums, clarinet, bass guitar, lead guitar, saxophone and keyboard/piano for worship services or other public functions is the core responsibility of an instrumentalist..

Experience:
You must be very vast and talented and possess a professional edge in playing of any of the above instruments. You should be able to transfer the skill by training others when the need arises. You have to be very skilled and creative,

Qualification
No set academic qualifications for entry into this job. Ability to flow very well with different sets of people particularly in a large choir or group is crucial to your success.

18. LAUNDRY/DRY CLEANING

Caring for fabrics or laundry and dry cleaning, as it is fondly called, is a serious, profitable but challenging business.

Fabric care, which involves laundry and dry cleaning, ironing and sometimes dyeing, is a delicate business to venture into, though it appears simple. It is a business which you can start, either on a small or middle scale and still post good profit.

How to start
The first step into the dry cleaning business is to have the passion and drive for it and be attentive to the smallest detail. Though capital is a key factor in setting up a dry cleaning business, one can start in a little way and then grow from there.

However, one needs to acquire some basic skills before one venture into the dry cleaning business. This is because dealing with people's clothes can be a very delicate endeavour and one needs to be careful, so as not to damage or deface the fabrics. One should also put the choice of location into serious consideration.

Education and Training Requirements
There are no educational requirements for many dry cleaning jobs. Most dry cleaning workers learn on the job, some trade schools and vocational schools offer courses in dry cleaning, finishing and spotting. The job takes only a few days to learn.

19. CATERING SERVICES
Catering involves the production, supply and service of food and drinks to guests at parties or events. Many different events require catering, from corporate or commercial to weddings and parties, and catering involves supplying these events with the food and drink required.

Responsibilities
Caterers are in charge of the food and drink, and this is a key element at many functions. People often remember the food; therefore delivering good quality service can make or mar a party. The range of what is required varies greatly and some parties require only cold snacks such as sandwiches, meat pies, cakes etc, but there are more extensive responsibilities, including serving full dinner with various courses, and dessert.

Qualifications
Formal qualifications are not strictly required for catering, which relies more on the ability to produce and deliver good food. However, the business and organisational aspects of the job may be made much easier with some teaching. There are standard catering schools everywhere for you to gain the requisite knowledge about the hospitality industry.

Skills
Caterers need a passion and flair for good food and the organisational and business skills to deliver that food to

large numbers of people, on time and in good condition. This means being a flexible cook, being prepared to meet the demands of a client, and having a good sense of cost, customer service and hospitality.

Catering operations are run as private businesses and many caterers are therefore self-employed. This involves a range of separate skills including managing accounts, dealing with people, maintaining a contact list and working in a team to deliver a professional and consistent service. If your are passionate about cooking, you can consider catering as a career.

20. HAIR AND SALOON BUSINESS

People seek beauty. They are constantly looking to improve what they have or give themselves a whole new look. It is no wonder that hair and salon business remains one of the rapidly growing industries today.

People drop by the nearest hair and beauty salon to be pampered by stylists and beauticians to style their tresses, shape their eyebrows, and colour their nails – all for a few (or more) naira. An hour in a hair and salon shop every month and one emerges confident and ready to take on the world.

Services Offered

Hair and salon businesses range from the haircut to upscale full-service hair, nail and day spa services that could pitch a price of a few hundred Naira.

A typical full-service hair and salon business offers all or any of the following services:

Hair Services
- haircuts, trims and style;
- highlights/foils and weaving;
- hair and scalp treatment;

- relaxers, perms and colours;
- shampoo and conditioning;
- curling, reconstructing and permanent weaving

Nails services
Manicure, pedicure, polish, sculptured nails, nail repair, hand conditioning treatment.

Skin Care
Facials, body waxing and massage.

Sale of professional hair/beauty products
Many salon businesses also offer a wide range of hair and beauty products in order to provide everything a customer needs in one convenient location. You can choose to sell top-of-the-line beauty products shampoo, daily and deep treatment conditioners, hair styling products such as mousse, gel, pomades among others; and other specialty hair products. Retailing professional hair products is an important strategy for retaining clients and making additional profits.

Some hair and salon businesses also offer spa services, a growing niche in the salon business. Day spas offer services such as body scrubs, skin lightening, body wrapping, herbal wraps, massage/aromatherapy, derma abrasion, stretch mark and blemishes, anti-aging, facials, makeup, skin care, waxing, polishing and anti-acne treatments.

21. MAKEUP ARTIST

"The best thing is to look natural, but it takes makeup to look natural"
- Calvin Klein.

This cute quote drives home the reason why many women cannot do without make-up. There are professional who help women and some men become more beautiful, by applying makeup. They are called makeup artists.

A makeup stylist - more commonly referred to as a makeup artist is someone who uses cosmetic techniques and processes to create beauty or fantasy with the human body.

In its simplest form, makeup artistry enhances a person's appearance, bringing out colour and features and hiding or smoothing out flaws. At its most extreme, makeup artistry creates imaginative characters and special effects for actors and actresses.

Basic requirement
A love of cosmetics and all the things they can do is one of the first signs of a budding makeup artist. If you like to experiment with different "looks" and to try them out on your friends, you may discover a real knack for applying makeup.

There are makeup artist schools which offer classes in all the different kinds of makeup.

A degree is not required, but a portfolio is essential.
The following industries with is in increasing demand for make-up artists

- Fashion Shows
- Modeling Agencies
- Magazines and other Publications
- Movies, Television, Theatre, Music Videos
- Advertising and
- Bridal Make-up

A make-up artist can also work independently. He/she can begin with an independent beauty salon that has the best of facilities and the latest trends in the beauty departments. The opportunities for a career in the make-up and beauty industry are many. Arm yourself with loads of creativity, a zest for new opportunities, an ability to improvise and a never-ending flow of ideas for a bright career as a make-up artist. There would surely be no dearth of opportunities heading your way!

BRIDAL MAKEUP ARTIST
The wedding day may be one of the most photographed and recorded events in a bride's life. For an event that has such significance, some brides hire the services of a professional makeup artist to ensure they look their best throughout the wedding ceremony and celebration. A career as a bridal makeup artist requires skill and training in makeup techniques as well as the charisma to work with nervous brides.

Build a Portfolio
A portfolio is an essential tool for a bridal makeup artist. Take good pictures of your work as you go from one project to another. The portfolio contains photographs of the makeup artist's work, which demonstrates proficiency, skill and style. Collaborating with wedding photographers could allow makeup artists to obtain professional photographs. Both the photographer and makeup artist can use the photographs in his or her portfolio. Friends and family members can be the subjects of the photographs.

22. RECHARGE CARDS BUSINESS
Those who still hold on to the popular catch phrase that "***talk is cheap***" are actually oblivious of the fact about the telecommunication industry and recharge card business.

One very vibrant business in Nigeria today is the recharge card business. It generates an estimated of ₦1 billion daily!

Wake up! Take This Job!

The recharge card printing business is a multi-million Naira business in Nigeria.

Over 5 million recharge cards are printed daily and those printing them make millions from the business. The good news is that now you can get your share of this money by joining the recharge card printing revolution.

All that you need to do for a start is to walk into the office of any of the network providers and tell them that you want to be involved in the sales and distribution of recharge card, I am sure they will give you all the necessary information that you need.

23. RECRUITING HOUSE CLEANER FOR PEOPLE

No matter how bad the economy, some people will pay to avoid housework. I am not talking about rich people only; even average people will pay to have their house clean. Cleaning houses is a very good way to create a strong relationship that could be of help to you in future.

Responsibilities:

Recruiting house cleaner for people who do not enjoy housework or do not have enough time to do it for themselves is a good business.

Basically, the job is to mop the floor, do the laundry and clean the entire house from kitchen to bedroom and in some cases take care of the kids. The moderate startup cost is for basic cleaning supplies such as sponges, mops and buckets. The schedule of the house cleaner depends on the needs of the client and could vary from once a week to once a month.

Qualifications:

Wake up! Take This Job!

You should be in the lookout for Neat, honest and God-fearing, individual with an eye for detail as a recruit for this service.

24. NETWORK MARKETING

Network marketing is a form of business that relies on person-to-person sales and recruiting. Individuals who earn a small profit from each sale sell products and services directly to consumers.

These same people recruit more people to invest in the products and sell them. A trickle effect ensues as members of each team build their own sub-teams and everyone earns residuals off the people they sign up

FIVE FUNDAMENTALS OF NETWORK MARKETING

i. **Product choice**: Choose a product that is easily stored and moved by the sales team. One of the benefits of network distribution systems is that you do not need brick and mortar sales centres or stores.

ii. **Team recruitment**: Recruit a core team of passionate salespeople. Ask your sales staff to pitch the product to people they already know and encourage their friends and family to join too. Your first line of sellers and recruiters will set the tone for the company and will make the difference in the speed with which your business grows.

iii. **Cheap Product kit**: Make sure the product sample kit is not too expensive for the salespeople to purchase.

iv. **Keep top recruiters in the circle**. While network marketing gives business people flexibility and independence, you will want to set up a solid and regular line of communications to maintain enthusiasm. Hold regular meetings and gatherings where they can share their experiences and success stories with their peers.

v. **Set up a payment system:** Set up a fair and equitable commission and residual payment structure that will serve to retain your top performers. Many network-marketing people start in the business part-time and as they see bigger profits, will turn their full-time efforts toward your company's success.

Provide regular opportunities for all members in the chain to join together. Annual conventions, seminar, conferences or quarterly meetings are great opportunities to highlight their work and encourage them to do more.

25. BEAD MAKING

Bead making has become a very profitable venture in our society today. If you have taken your time to look around, especially at wedding, burial or naming ceremonies, you will notice different designs of beads especially on the ladies.

The beads come in different colours, shapes and sizes. Beads are usually worn for beautification and fashion purposes especially by ladies.

Bead making in the last decade has experienced a market boom because of the paradigm shift in fashion style amongst the ladies. Beads have gradually replaced gold and silver necklaces and bangles.

What you make with beads
There are a lot of things that can be made with beads, and new discoveries are springing up every day. Last Christmas a friend told me that he saw a "Father Christmas" that was made with beads.

So you can agree with me that the opportunities in bead making are endless.

Wake up! Take This Job!

Things that can be done with beads includes bags, belts, shoes, flower vase, necklace, ear rings, play toys, Rings, table cloth, wrist watches, bangles, handset carriers, wallets, purse, crowns, and traditional caps.

These twenty five jobs are by no means the only ordinary jobs with extraordinary potentials; they are written here so that your mind can be open to think, your eyes open to see and your hands and feet provoked to take action.

Wake up! Take This Job!

CHAPTER 15

"Sometimes doing your best is not good enough. Sometimes you must do what is required."
-Winston Churchill

CHAPTER FIFTEEN

INDISPENSABLE REQUIREMENTS FOR ALL ORDINARY JOB PROVIDERS

With what we have discussed so far, I believe you are already fired up to start working. Before you start, there are some requirement that must be in place for your success to be guaranteed.

TWELVE INDISPENSABLE REQUIREMENTS FOR ALL ORDINARY JOB PROVIDERS

1. **Character**

"Be more concerned about your character than your reputation, because your character is what you really are, while your reputation is merely what others think you are."
-John Wooden

Character is an indispensable asset when it comes to doing ordinary jobs and it is a key advertising tool. Character stands tall in the world of business. Nobody does business with a person of questionable character. You must be trustworthy, honest and be a person of your word.

A man's character is the reality of himself"

Wake up! Take This Job!

-H.W. Beecher

2. Know your skills

"Knowing something is confidence, doing it well is competence"
-John C. Maxwell

Next to character is skill. What kind of job are you skilled at and are willing to do? Lots of jobs do not require any special knowledge or skill. Most people can take pictures, wash their clothes and even paint a wall, what matters is to strive to be the best at whatever you do.

If you have special skills or attributes, you could charge a little more for special jobs. Can you fix cars? Help someone build a website? Tutor Math? Use your skills to make money. A man's skill makes run for him. Your skill must be sharpened so that the services you render will showcase excellence. People do not appreciate shoddy services.

3. Dress Properly

"Dress the way you wish to be addressed"
-Archbishop B.A.Idahosa

Your personal appearance is not only an important factor in how you present yourself to others; the way you dress reflects the importance you attach to the situation and people around you. If your clothes are unclean or wrinkled, you may appear to be careless and uninterested in the business situation or people you are interacting with.

Someone once told me this and it stuck, "I dress to the level I want to achieve." So, if you want to be CEO, think about how you look when you leave the house in the morning. Do you carry yourself like an executive? Do not forget this English proverb: *"**the apparel proclaims the man.**"*

Here is a basic rule of thumb you can follow:

- When meeting with business associates or clients, whether in your office or theirs, you should dress appropriately — if they wear suits, you should wear one.

All business attire, whether traditional or casual, should be reflective of a professional, dignified appearance.

"Great men are seldom over-scrupulous in the arrangement of their attire"
-Charles Dickens

4. Know your market

Who are the people that require your services? Where are they located?

- Is there a population of senior citizens in your area?
- Are there people living around you that have retired from active service? Anyone who is trustworthy and reliable can make a living helping seniors and retirees.
- Are there lots of young families in your area? Parents need childcare and tutoring for their children.
- Is your area filled with busy professionals and career persons? They may need dry cleaners to take care of their laundry or home maintenance that they do not have time for.
- Are there young school leavers in your area? You may start up extra mural classes to prepare them for JAMB and Post UME examinations.

You must have a specific group of people that you are targeting. For instance, this book has a specific target market: the teeming unemployed youth. It is specific. Target your market wisely and your success will be sure.

5. Promote yourself

Market yourself. People have to know that you do what you do. Do not be ashamed of what you do. Make up some fliers and business cards. You can use programmes like Microsoft Word or Publisher, or if you can afford a graphic designer, get one to design a business card for you. Include your name or the name of your business, your phone number and list the jobs you are willing to do, any special skills that you have and the cities you are willing to travel to.

Pass the fliers or posters out around the neighborhood, at football viewing centres, in the church and everywhere you go. Place your advert in church bulletin with your phone number; in most churches, it is free of charge.

Every conversation is an opportunity for you to market yourself. Find a way to chip in your business during conversation. When you talk about it with passion, people will believe you.

6. Advertise online

One of the best means to get the word out is to advertise online. Use Facebook, Twitter and other social network to spread the news about yourself. If you can create a blog, go ahead and create one, but if not, then use the social networks extensively. It is free. Post your advert (picture, posters and fliers) on your Facebook page. Also try to respond to inquiries promptly.

7. Knock On Doors
Do not be afraid to go out there and introduce yourself to the people in your community. Do not do a hard sell, just say hello, tell them your name and what you do, give them a flier or business card and thank them for their time. People appreciate someone who is friendly and informative. They will not appreciate someone who is pushy and will be inclined to mistrust a hard sell.

This particular strategy works like magic, there are lots of people out there that are not just willing to give you a job but are ready to help you succeed.

When I finished my NYSC, I came back broke and with nobody to help but before I left for service, I had started my first book "***The Compendium of Wisdom***". I sat down and thought of what to do with the book. I decided to go out into the city and get people to make written contributions to the book. The response I got was unprecedented. People wrote quotes, recommended others and the book was completed.

At the end, most of the people became my mentors, I could walk up to their offices and say, "Sir", "Ma" I am about to do this or that, I need your support and they will gladly give it. It started when I stepped out of the house and knocked on the doors of their offices.

8. Organisation/Scheduling Of Tasks
Learn to prioritise tasks and organise a 'convenient' schedule that allows you to carry out a maximum number of jobs in a minimal time period. If one task takes you to a certain part of town, schedule all other tasks that can be covered around the same area along with that task. This will save you a lot of time, transport fare and energy. You will need to learn the art of

prioritising for you to meet the demands of all your clients as at when due.

9. Build Your Business:
Great things start from small beginning. You must have a vision, the extent to which what you choose to do will grow depends on the size of your vision. Where you are now is just the first rung on the ladder, you still have a long way to go. Always have the picture of where you are going in mind.

Grow and protect your reputation Ask people you have worked for if you could use them for a recommendation, and to spread the word about your services and reliability. Word of mouth is often the very best form of advertisement. People will trust the word of someone they know easier than someone they do not know. Most importantly, be honest and reliable and you will probably have more job offers than you can handle.

10. Render Excellent Services
The revered Greek philosopher and polymath, Aristotle who lived between (384-322 BC) would probably be talking to an ordinary job provider when he (in one of his many great thoughts about excellence) wrote:

"Excellence is an art won by training and habituation. We do not act rightly because we have virtue or excellence, but we rather have those because we acted rightly. We are what we repeatedly do. Excellence then is not an act, but a habit."

You must develop the habit of rendering quality and excellent jobs. Your motto should be passion for excellence. People are tired of substandard, run-off-the-mill services. Whatever you do, let it be the best. If people are looking for the best hair dresser, your name should pop up in their minds; if people are looking for the best painter, your name should readily come to mind. Be outstanding and stand out from the crowd. Be the best and not second best.

11.   Keep good records
Make sure you keep accurate records. Keep a client record of names, telephone numbers, addresses and jobs you have done. Give honest, accurate estimates and give receipts when necessary. Also when necessary write up a simple contract, even if the job is small. This tells the person that you are a legitimate business person that they can rely on. It will also save you a lot of headaches if there is ever a dispute over a job.

Record keeping does not only help you track your progress, it saves you from many unforeseen troubles. You never can tell what will crop up if you do not keep records. Someone could accuse you of not having delivered goods or rendered a service that you have already done. Such accusation, if not properly handled could cripple your emerging business. The easiest way is to bring out your record book and show it to the person concerned and the matter will be laid to rest.

12.   Be Profit Oriented-Always Charge A Fee
The purpose of business is to make profit. Remember your main objective is to generate income. Always charge a fee for whatever job you do, no matter how small, except you are doing it for charity.

As a business person, charging a fee is as important as the air you breathe. Quote your prices based on the services you offer. Charge your clients a reasonable rate for your services. Finding a reasonable rate can be difficult but try not to charge too little for your time. Work out how long each job will take and set your price

Wake up! Take This Job!

accordingly, taking into account any equipment you may also need to purchase or hire.

ACTION, NOT JUST THINKING PRODUCES RESULT
We have said a lot about the ordinary jobs, now what more can we say? I will express it in a six letter word A-C-T-I-O-N. Take action now!

Wake up! Take This Job!

CHAPTER 16

"The gains of life accrues to those who are engaged in doing something worthwhile with their life"

-Samuel Aghomi

CHAPTER SIXTEEN
THE GAINS OF ENGAGING IN ORDINARY JOBS

1. You Have Money In Your Pocket

Money gives you confidence. By engaging in common jobs you are sure of having money in your pocket and keeping your confidence level high. By doing some of the so-called ordinary jobs/businesses you are in charge of your income. You decide what you earn. This can be seen as a pro or a con at first, but eventually the sky will be the limit as you develop your business.

In the beginning, seeking self-employment by doing the common jobs might not fetch you as much as you need, the huge advantage is the fact that you keep everything that you make and your salary is not determined by your employer.

2. You are the CEO
Answering to a boss is normal protocol when working and having to report to a boss could be demanding to say the least. Doing the common jobs allows you to be your own boss and takes away much of the stress of working a regular job. When you are the boss, although you'll still have deadlines and obligations to meet, you are the only person you'll have to answer to. Most

common jobs do not involve demanding clients and customers, so you typically do not have to worry about them bossing you around either. You are the Chief Executive Officer (CEO)

3. Experience

"Experience is not what happens to a man; it is what a man does with what happens to him."
-Aldous Huxley

Life is a continuous chain of experiences. Experience is the key element to being successful at a job or earning a more desired job. Prospective employers are going to be looking very closely at your CV to see why they should employ you and not someone else. They will want to see experience. Life experience, not classroom experience,

Your academic qualifications are important but most employers care more about your ability to use you education, than they do about your successful memorization of text books to pass exams. It helps to have some experience under your belt as you seek for better jobs.

How do you get experience when no one will give you a chance? By doing the ordinary jobs you actually gain experience that you probably will not get if you stay without doing anything worthwhile.

A successful period of Work Experience in doing the ordinary jobs will not only look good on your CV but it can also be a stepping stone for future employment.

Doing ordinary jobs requires you to develop skills and techniques to achieve a successful working relationship. It may be that the job you are doing will bring you into contact with clients and members of the public, where other skills are required.

4. Network

It is believed that your networks determine your net worth. When people work they have a wonderful chance to meet other people and communicate with them. It is so important to be sociable and to be able to work with different category of people. Ordinary job help you make new relations and networks that can lead you to your destination faster.

5. A Platform To Start Your Own Small Business

You can start a small business doing ordinary jobs for people. As long as there are people who need things done for them, you can make money. Simply provide a service that people need.

Many multi-million naira businesses have been started this way. There are always people out there who need something done and some people either do not have the time, the knowledge, or the physical ability to do it.

Engaging in a common job not only puts money in your pocket but creates a platform for you to actually start your dream business.

6. Flexibility

When you are involved in the common jobs, you enjoy the flexibility of setting your own schedule. You set your own hours and work when it is convenient for you. This provides more time for other activities. Having an ordinary job or business allows you to enjoy the freedom and flexibility you never thought you could afford.

7. Sharpen your skill

People improve their skills while they are working. If you want to be a professional in any field or sphere you should work hard and improve your skills every day. If a person wants to be famous and successful, he or she

Wake up! Take This Job!

has to work hard. So this is one more reason why you should take up the ordinary job. It enables you to sharpen your entrepreneurial skill and develop a business person's mindset.

DISRUPT THE STATUS QUO!
Ideas are not enough.
You must be action oriented to improve your future
Do not just think but act.
You get results not only from thinking but from acting
You have ideas.
You want to achieve. You want opportunity.
But what are you still doing in your comfort zone?
The comfort zone is a dangerous place to be.
"I planned to", "I wanted to", "I was going to" cannot put on a light bulb, not to talk of moving you forward.
Are you not tired of hoping and criticising?
Stop defending the status quo that locks you down.
Go on the offensive now with your new knowledge of the potentials of the so-called ordinary jobs
What is the use of ideas without action?
What is the use of acquiring knowledge with doing something with it?
Start becoming the achiever you deserve to be.
MAKE SURE THERE IS NO STANDING ROOM FOR EXCUSES.

<u>Wake up! Take This Job!</u>

FINAL WORD
LOOK IN THE MIRROR
"A man becomes what he consistently beholds"

As I begin to draw the curtain on this book I particularly want you to know that we live in a time of great uncertainty but amidst all the uncertainties, you can find solace. You can find calm amidst the storm. There are two ways you can find you away around in times like this:

i. standing on a new platform, and
ii. looking at the divine mirror

Standing On the platform of divinity
So many young people out there are standing on the wrong platform, such as: the platform of government promises, family background, institution attended, grades acquired from the University and so on. Because they stand on these shaky platforms, all they have consistently seen are the same things: the reality of unemployment, failed promises and the failing economy. When you stand on the wrong platform, you cannot get the right perspective and without the right perspective, you cannot get the right outcome.

There is a platform on which you can stand and view the world around you. This platform is high above all other; it is solid and provides a vantage point for you to have a clear and an uncluttered view of the world. This platform is **the dais of divinity**-The platform of what God said in the Holy Scripture.

I do not want to sound religious, but the truth is that, if you do not see the world from God's angle, you cannot get the right perspective.

The scripture says in Isaiah 55:8-9 (KJV)
"For my thoughts are not your thoughts, neither are your ways my ways saith the Lord. For as the heavens are higher than the earth, so are my ways higher than your ways, and my thoughts than your thoughts."

When you stand on the path that God has blazed, you will see things differently. People that are standing on the right path-God path always see light amidst darkness, possibility amidst impossibility, peace amidst crisis-they see a different picture because they are standing on a different platform and are looking in a different direction from the rest of the world.

While the world is looking up to their various governments, those standing on the **"dais of divinity"**, which is represented by Jesus Christ are looking upward. Government can fail but they that look up to the Lord will never be brought to shame.

The divine mirror

When you are standing on the new dais, you must keep your gaze fixed on the divine mirror, the mirror of the word of God. God's vision for the world is embedded in the word; His vision for your life is trapped in the Holy Scripture - His word. If you want to see what He wants you to be, then keep your eyes on the mirror, the divine mirror-the Word of God.

If you continue to look in the mirror, you will see a new picture, a picture of the person you ought to be, a picture that is so glorious, so distinct, so different from

Wake up! Take This Job!

your present image. If you continue to look in the mirror, you will not only see your true self, you will with time become what you see in the mirror.

For the scripture says in 2 Corinthians 4: 18

"but we all with open face beholding as in a glass, the glory of the Lord, are changed into the same image from glory to glory, even as by the Spirit of the Lord."

You become what you behold. When you become what you see in the mirror, we say you have been transformed by the Word of God. Once you are transformed, you will see the world different; your perception would have been altered completely.

It all begins when you accept Jesus as the Lord of your life. You can do it now!

Just say this short prayer:

Lord Jesus, I accept you today, as my Lord and my personal saviour, forgive me my sisn and wash me with your precious blood. I believe, you died for me and on the third day you rose again for my justification.
Right now I believe I am saved from sin and Satan to serve the living God.
Thank you Jesus for saving me.

Welcome to the family of God. Congratulation!

FOR COUNSELLING PLEASE CALL:
08074848825
or
Email: samaghomi@gmail.com

REFERENCES

Craig, J. and Dawn J. (2000). *E-Business Readiness*. 1st ed'. Addison-Wesley Professional.

Covey, S. (2006) Everyday *Greatness.* New York, Rutledge Hill Press

Doyle, A. C. (1887) *A Study In Scarlet.* Ward, Lock and Co. UK

Egba, S. P. (2010): *The Impact of Business Studies in Schools. A Hand Book on Practical Business in Schools*. Port Harcourt. Akpos Learning Publishers,

EU YOUTH REPORT, SEC (2009) Youth - Investing and Empowering" 549 final.
http://www.un.org/esa/socdev/youthemployment/yenpr.doc

Gee, J. & Gee, V. (2006), *The Winner's Attitude: Change How You Deal with Difficult People and Get the BEST Out of Any Situation.* New York: McGraw-Hill companies.

Harrell, K. (2003), *The Attitude is everything Workbook: Strategies and Tools for Developing Personal and Professional Success.* New York: HarperCollins Publishers Inc.

Kenyon, P. and White, S. (2001): *Enterprise-based youth employment policies, strategies and programmes*, International Labour Office, Geneva, p. 7.

Kiyosaki, R. (1999) *Retire Young, Retire Rich.* New York, Warner Books Inc.

MacOliver F.O, Okafor F.C., Nwagu N.A., Okojie C.E.E (2006) **"Entrepreneurship Development: The Nigerian Experience***".* Benin City. Mareh Publishers.

Wake up! Take This Job!

Maxwell, J. C. (1993), *The Winning Attitude*. Nashville, Tennessee: Thomas Nelson, Inc.

Nneji S.P (1999) The Impact of Business in Nigeria, *Pearl Journal of Business & Management*, Vol.6, No. 2 Page 6-12.

Nsubuga, William, M. (2008) *The role of attitude inside and outside toady's organisation.* Master's Thesis in MBA. University of Boras Http://hdl.handle.net/2320/3942

OECD definition cited by Cynthia Hewitt De Alcántara (2001): *The Development Divide in a Digital Age: An Issues Paper*, UNRISD, Technology, Business and Society Programme Paper Number 4, August 2001, United Nations Research Institute for Social Development, Geneva , p. 3.(8)

Oladunjoye, I.N (2007): *"The principle of Business Studies"* Ola Printing House, Lagos.

Park, W.R and Park S.C(1978). **How To Succeed In You Business,** John Wiley and Sons, Chichester.

Paul Timmers, (2000), Electronic Commerce - strategies & models for business-to-business trading, , John Wiley & Sons, Ltd,

Popoola, A. T. (2012) The Job Creation Imperative of job. *First Bank Review -A Semi-Annual Journal of Business and the Economy* Vol. 2. Iss. 1. Pg 34.

Robbins, A. (1991) *Awakening the Giant within You*. New York. The Free Press-Simon Schuster, Inc.

Romer, P., (1990) Endogenous Technological Change, *Journal of Political Economy*, 98:5 11

Selwyn, N. (2002), Defining the *'Digital Divide'*: developing a theoretical understanding of inequalities in the information age.
http://www.cf.ac.uk/socsi/ict/definingdigitaldivide.pdf

Steve V. Willard, T., and Maja A. (2005) A Developing Connection: Bridging the Policy Gap between the Information Society and Sustainable Development.. '1st ed'. Canada: IISD, (9)

UdonKang E.C. (2002): Comparative Studies of Business Education and other Discipline in Nigeria. *Ekpo Educational Journal.* Vol. 7, No. 10, Pg 6-7.

UNESCO (1997) *Environment and Society: Education and public awareness for sustainability*, Background Paper prepared for UNESCO International Conference, Thessaloniki, 7.

Wikipedia (2009) Motivation. Web site:
http://en.wikipedia.org/wiki/motivation.

Wikipedia (2010), Job Performance. Web site:
http://en.wikipedia.org/wiki/jobperformance.

Wikipedia, 2010 online Encyclopedia http://en.wikipedia.org/

World Bank (2007). Case Studies - Empowerment through Information. http://go.worldbank.org/MYTEYM8A00.

Zig Ziglar (1986) *Top Performance.* New York The Berkley Publishing Group.

Zimmerman, A. R. (2006) *Pivot: How One Turn In Attitude Can Lead To Success.* Austin Texas: Peak Performance Publishers.

www.ingramcontent.com/pod-product-compliance
Lightning Source LLC
LaVergne TN
LVHW051727080426
835511LV00018B/2930